A Timeline of the Written Word

Hieroglyphics to Hypertext

WORLD BOOK

World Book
a Scott Fetzer company
Chicago

World Book, Inc.
180 North LaSalle Street
Suite 900
Chicago, Illinois 60601
USA

For information about other World Book publications, call 1-800-WORLDBK (967-5325).

For information about sales to schools and libraries, call 1-800-975-3250 (United States) or 1-800-837-5365 (Canada).

Produced for World Book, Inc. by Bailey Publishing Associates Ltd.

Library of Congress Cataloging-in-Publication Data

Title: Hieroglyphics to hypertext: a timeline of the written word.
Description: Chicago: World Book, Inc., a Scott Fetzer company, [2016] | Series: A timeline of ... | Includes index.
Identifiers: LCCN 2016012920 | ISBN 9780716635468
Subjects: LCSH: Writing--History--Juvenile literature. | Printing--History--Juvenile literature. | Books--History--Juvenile literature. | Written communication--History--Juvenile literature.
Classification: LCC Z40 .H54 2016 | DDC 411/.7--dc23
LC record available at https://lccn.loc.gov/2016012920

Hieroglyphics to Hypertext: A Timeline of the Written Word
ISBN: 978-0-7166-3546-8
A Timeline of... Set ISBN: 978-0-7166-3539-0
E-book ISBN: 978-0-7166-3555-0 (ePUB3 format)
Printed in China by Shenzhen Wing King Tong Paper Products Co., Ltd., Guangdong Province
1st printing July 2016

Acknowledgments

Cover photo: Shutterstock (song_mi).

Bildarchiv Austria 31.

Bridgeman 6 (Ancient Art & Architecture), 8 left (W. Forman), 12 (Stapleton), 13 right (De Morgan Foundation), 15, 17 (Z. Radovan), 18 (De Agostini), 19 left (British Museum), 19 right (PFH), 20 (Board of Trinity College), 25 left (Yale Center for British Art), 25 right (Tarker), 30 (Charmet), 33 (Stapleton).

Corbis 22 (Xu Yu/Xinhua Press).

Dvortygirl 36 right.

Getty 7 (M. Seemuller), 9 (De Agostini), 10 right, 14 (Express), 16 left, 21 left (UHA), 23 (UIG), 24 (R. Viollet), 26-27 (UHA), 29 left (T. Williams), 32 left (Science & Society), 32 right (Keystone), 34 (Bettmann), 36 left (Science & Society).

Ian Winton 8 right.

iStock 16 right (Matthias Ledwinka).

Luca 10 left.

Neoneo13 21 right.

Shutterstock 4 top (Kokhanchikov), 4 bottom (Giakita), 11 (Infografx), 13 left (f. de marco), 28 (C. Mueller), 35 (tomgigabite), 37 (Andrey_Popov).

Solipsist 29 right.

Glossary There is a glossary of terms on page 38. Terms defined in the glossary are in type that **looks like this** (called *boldface type*) on their first appearance on any *spread* (two facing pages).

Circa Some dates are written with *c.* before the year. The *c.* stands for *circa.* Circa means *approximately.* For example, with c. 250 B.C., the phrase is read as "circa 250 B.C.," meaning *approximately 250 B.C.* Circa can be used with both B.C. and A.D. dates.

Contents

Hieroglyphics to Hypertext

A Timeline of the Written Word

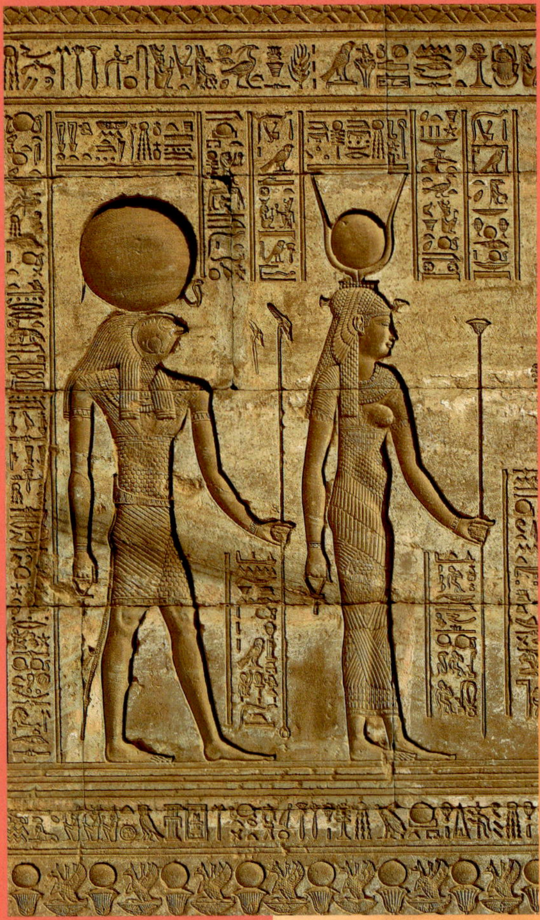

An early form of writing known as **hieroglyphics** developed in ancient Egypt around 3200 B.C.

Today, many people read on e-readers. E-readers carry hundreds of **e-books** on one convenient, portable electronic device.

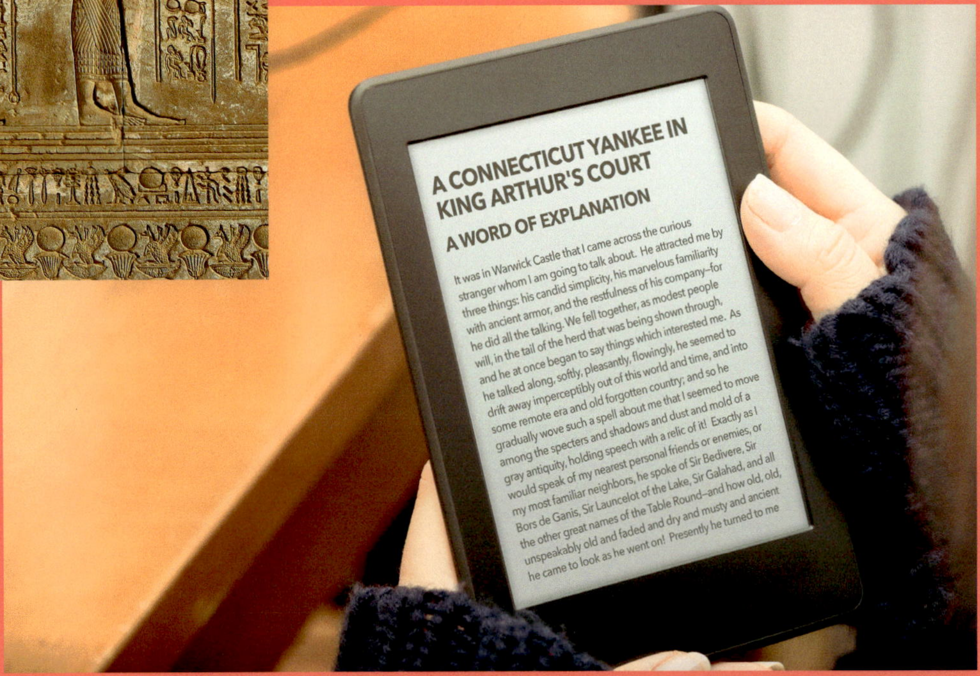

Introduction

Writing Through the Ages

Before writing, people communicated through speech and hand signals. There was no method to write down stories, send messages, or keep written records. Around 5,000 years ago, in the part of the world we know as the Middle East, people drew pictures to stand for spoken words. They invented writing. With writing, humans could send messages over long distances and preserve ideas across generations. Writing helped to spread information and new ideas across the world.

Over time, writing systems became easier to learn and use. Early writing used pictures and symbols to represent objects and ideas. Later, people developed symbols to represent the sounds of speech. These sound symbols became the first **alphabet** letters.

People also invented different ways to record writing. For centuries, people carved writing into clay tablets and other surfaces. The Egyptians invented a new writing surface called **papyrus.** Papyrus is an early type of paper that could be written on and rolled into scrolls. Later civilizations made **parchment** and then developed paper. Books, with sturdy bindings and covers, replaced fragile scrolls.

For many centuries, books were rare and expensive. The invention of the printing press made books easier to create and less expensive to buy. Such cultural movements as the **Renaissance** and the **Reformation** were influenced by printed materials.

The invention of computers, keyboards, and electronic, or digital, text greatly changed the way people read and write. Today, many people read digital copies of books, called **e-books,** on e-readers instead of paper books. Other people write by typing on a keyboard instead of handwriting on paper. Although writing and printing have changed over time, their function remains the same—to communicate, inform, inspire, and entertain.

To learn more, follow the timeline through this book to trace the history of writing and printing from the earliest civilizations to the present day.

Chapter 1

Ancient Writing Systems

c. 3300 B.C.—c. 2300 B.C.

The first writing system was developed by a group of people called the Sumerians, who lived in southern Mesopotamia in what is now the nation of Iraq. They drew pictures to stand for words. These symbols are known as **pictograms.**

Pictograms are useful for expressing such words as *fish*, *person*, or *house*. These things can be easily drawn as pictures. But it is harder to express ideas, thoughts, and feelings using pictures. Another problem with using pictograms as a writing

c. 3300 B.C.

The Sumerians developed symbols we now call pictograms.

c. 3200 B.C.

People in ancient Egypt developed a picture writing system called **hieroglyphics.** Sometimes their pictures stood for an object or idea. In other cases, the pictures stood for words, parts of words, or numbers. The ancient Egyptians used hieroglyphic writing for more than 3,000 years (later form of writing below).

The Egyptians also invented an early form of paper called **papyrus.** This early paper was made from the papyrus plant, which grew near the Nile River. To make papyrus, strips of the plant's stem were laid on top of one another. Then pressure was applied to the layers. This pressure crushed the strips together to form a rough, white paper. The Egyptians wrote on papyrus using inks made from such materials as berries, bark, and soot.

system is that each individual object or idea needs its own unique picture. Early Sumerian writing probably had more than 2,000 pictograms. The large amount of pictograms made this writing hard to learn.

The Sumerians eventually found a solution to these problems. They used pictograms to stand for sounds of human speech, not just objects or ideas. By around 2600 B.C., **cuneiform** writing had begun to use both pictograms and phonograms—signs that represented sounds. The Sumerians made use of homonyms. For example, the word *ti* in Sumerian meant both *arrow* and *life*. They drew an arrow for both meanings, with extra pictures when the meaning was *life*. They created a syllabary—a list of symbols, each of which represented a syllable.

Sargon of Akkad and his military conquered Mesopotamia. He ruled from 2334 B.C. to 2279 B.C. The conquerors spoke Akkadian, a different language than Sumerian. But, the Akkadians preserved much of the Sumerians' culture, including their cuneiform writing system. Many later cultures that lived in Mesopotamia also used cuneiform, including the Babylonians, Canaanites, Hittites, Assyrians, and Persians.

c. 2300 B.C.

The Sumerians used small, sharp sticks to press wedge-shaped marks into wet clay tablets. This type of writing is called *cuneiform* (*kyoo NEE uh fawrm*). Many of the marks represent words or syllables. When the writing was complete, the clay tablet was dried in the sun. This drying method hardened the clay and preserved the writing upon it. Cuneiform was used for more than 3,000 years (later form of writing above).

c. 3000 B.C.

Chapter 2

Early Alphabets and Texts

c. 2000 B.C.—c. 800 B.C.

Learning to write in **cuneiform** and **hieroglyphics** was extremely difficult. These systems used hundreds of individual pictures and symbols. Few people could use the writing systems. Only experts with many years of training knew all of the symbols' meanings.

The next great advance in writing, the **alphabet,** brought written script closer to spoken language. Scholars believe that Semite workers in ancient Egypt invented the first alphabet in the 1800's B.C. Semites were people who spoke

c. 2000 B.C.

The *Epic of Gilgamesh* is one of the world's earliest known works of literature. It is an **epic** poem about a powerful Sumerian king named Gilgamesh. Saddened by the death of a friend, Gilgamesh searches for the secret to eternal life. He fails in his quest. But the walls of Gilgamesh's great city, Uruk, are inscribed with his name. This Babylonian *seal* (an object that leaves a mark when pressed into another material) shows a picture of Gilgamesh holding a lion.

c. 1800's B.C.

The earliest writing using an alphabet dates from around the 1800's B.C. Scholars call this writing system *Proto-Sinaitic.* This writing system was probably invented by Semites working in ancient Egypt. These workers adapted the complex Egyptian writing system into a system of just 27 letters. The Proto-Sinaitic alphabet only had consonants. There were no vowels. When two letters were put side-by-side, such as *ts* or *sh*, they stood for another sound.

Word	Proto-Sinaitic
'alp ("ox")	
mem ("water")	
'en ("eye")	

languages related to modern Hebrew and Arabic. The Akkadians and Babylonians were Semites. So were the Canaanites, who lived along the eastern coast of the Mediterranean Sea, just west of Mesopotamia and north of Egypt.

Semite workers in Egypt were probably familiar with Egyptian hieroglyphs. They realized that one hieroglyphic symbol could be used to write one sound, instead of one symbol representing a whole word. For example, a wavy line hieroglyph stood for the word *water*. The word for *water* is *mem* in Semitic language. So, the Semites used a wavy line symbol to stand for the "m" sound.

Eventually, 27 symbols came into use. Each symbol represented a speech sound. These symbols were the beginning of the alphabet.

c. 1750 B.C.

The *Code of Hammurabi* is one of the earliest surviving sets of laws. It was carved onto clay tablets. Hammurabi (?-1750 B.C.) was the king of Babylon, an area in what is now Iraq. His code was written in Akkadian cuneiform.

c. 1500 B.C.

The earliest known **parchment** scrolls date from about 1500 B.C. For early writers, it had advantages over **papyrus.** Made from dried animal skins, parchment was more durable, did not rot in damp or wet conditions, and could be scraped clean and reused. Long pieces of parchment could be rolled up. However, parchment was expensive to buy and heavy to carry.

Early Alphabets and Texts

c. 2000 B.C.—c. 800 B.C.

The **alphabet** did not immediately replace **cuneiform** and **hieroglyphics.** But the alphabet would eventually change writing systems around the world. Many cultures throughout Europe, Asia, and North Africa read and wrote with alphabets. Many centuries later, the printing press relied on alphabet letters.

The alphabet's spread began in Canaan. The Canaanites were neighbors to three great ancient civilizations—Mesopotamia, Egypt, and Greece. The Canaanites probably spoke a language much like modern Hebrew. Ancient Israel was a country in Canaan.

c. 1400's B.C.

People in Canaan used an alphabet sometimes called *Proto-Canaanite.*

c. 1000 B.C.

Proto-Canaanite letters developed into a system called the *Phoenician alphabet.* The Phoenician alphabet had 22 letters. The letters were named after objects. For example, the first letter was *alp*, meaning *ox.* This letter was shaped like an ox head. The second letter, *beyt,* meant *house.* It originally looked like a box-shaped home.

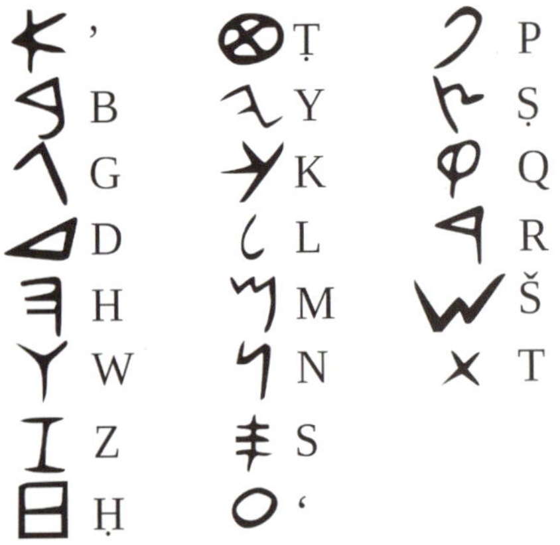

c. 900 B.C.

The Phoenician alphabet was easy to use for many of the Semitic languages spoken around the Mediterranean Sea. But by about 900 B.C., a Semitic language called *Aramaic* had its own version of the Phoenician alphabet. At this time, the powerful Assyrian Empire spoke Aramaic. The Assyrians still used cuneiform for many ceremonial purposes. But they used the Aramaic alphabet for daily business. Modern Arabic and Hebrew alphabets are based on the Aramaic alphabet. So are certain scripts of India and central Asia.

Some Canaanites were sailors and traders. They traded items around the Mediterranean Sea and were known for such red-purple dyed goods as cloth. The ancient Greeks called the Canaanites *Phoenicians*, from the Greek word for red-purple, *phoinix*.

By 1000 B.C., the Phoenicians' alphabet contained only 22 letters. Scholars call this version of the alphabet *Phoenician.* Through trade, the Phoenicians spread their alphabet to other lands. Eventually, the ancient Greeks began using the Phoenician alphabet. But the Greeks made a few important changes. They changed some letters into vowels. The Greek alphabet eventually developed into what is now known as the *Roman alphabet.* This book, like all English texts, is written with Roman alphabet letters.

The ancient Greeks learned the Phoenician alphabet from Phoenician traders. Greek is not a Semitic language. So the Greeks changed the Phoenician alphabet to fit their spoken language. The Greeks used certain Phoenician letters as vowels. They changed the shape of many letters. The Greeks also borrowed their letter names from the Phoenicians, but ignored the Semitic meanings. For example, *alp* became *alpha* in Greek. *Beyt* became *beta*. The Greeks put the words *alpha* and *beta* together to make the word *alphabet*. Also, Phoenician and Aramaic writing was read from right to left. Writing in Greek was read from left to right.

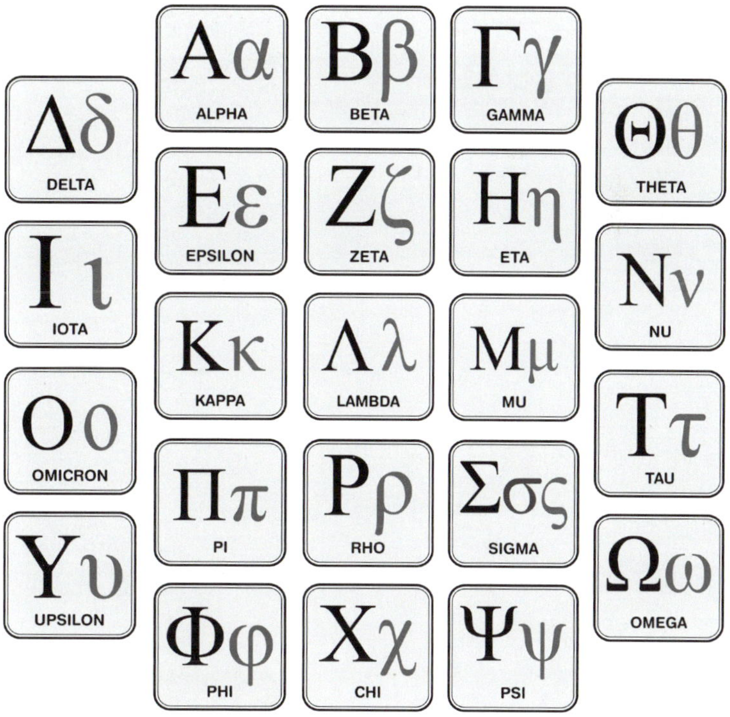

c. 800 B.C.

Chapter 3

How Writing Records History

700 B.C.—c. 200 B.C.

Writing is useful because it records knowledge and ideas. **Cuneiform** tablets contain the same words today as they did when they were made thousands of years ago. But most ancient writings were not so permanent. Few original texts that were written on **papyrus** or **parchment** survive today. Only copies of these original writings are available to us. Scholars must piece together past histories based upon the recorded copies.

In 704 B.C., Sennacherib became king of Assyria. He reigned from 704 B.C. to 681 B.C. Sennacherib founded a great library in the city of Nineveh, in what is now the country of Iraq. Decades later, Sennacherib's grandson, King Ashurbanipal who reigned from 668 B.C. to 627 B.C., founded another library nearby. Ashurbanipal gathered many clay tablets from earlier Mesopotamian cultures to put in his library. They included the *Epic of Gilgamesh* and other important Babylonian and Sumerian works. These tablets were kept safe within the library's walls.

704 B.C.

Many ancient texts document earlier *oral* (spoken) stories. The famous Greek **epic** poems, the *Iliad* and the *Odyssey*, were likely originally spoken, not written. Scholars believe these stories were first told in the 700's B.C. by a poet named Homer. Each new generation would have memorized the stories. But the stories probably changed over decades of retellings before they were ever written down.

Even when written, the *Iliad* and *Odyssey* continued to change over time. Writers who copied the text by hand made changes—sometimes by mistake and sometimes on purpose. By 300 B.C., many slightly different versions of these stories existed in Greece. Other important texts have similar histories. For example, many parts of the Hebrew Bible were originally oral traditions. Scholars believe they were written down centuries later.

c. 700 B.C.

The Etruscans, who lived in what is now central Italy, learned the Greek **alphabet** from Greek settlers living near the city of Naples. The Etruscans ruled a simple farming community named Rome. In time, the Romans grew more powerful. They rose up and drove out the Etruscans. They adjusted the Greek alphabet to fit their spoken language, Latin. The Romans eventually created a vast empire. The Latin language spread through western Europe—and so did the Latin alphabet.

587 B.C.

The Babylonians conquered the kingdom of Judah, in what is now Israel, capturing many Jewish leaders. During this period, called the *Babylonian Exile,* Jewish captives collected and expanded the Hebrew Bible text. Much of the material was told as oral stories before it was written down. Some books were rewritten by different people who composed new material and added other teachings to the earlier writings.

c. 550 B.C.

Scholars believe the *Iliad* and the *Odyssey* were first written down around this time.

How Writing Records History

700 B.C.—c. 200 B.C.

Many ancient scholars traveled far distances to study in the celebrated libraries of the ancient world. Some of the greatest philosophers and scientists spent much of their time in libraries. Ancient libraries were not like today's lending libraries. Their "books" looked nothing like modern books. The writings in ancient libraries were mostly on **papyrus** scrolls or clay tablets. Both writing surfaces were very delicate and could not be removed from the building. The scrolls and tablets held important information about the past. Aside from scholars, not many people used these libraries because most ancient people could not read.

c. 479 B.C.

Chinese philosopher Confucius (551? B.C.-479? B.C.) died. Shortly afterward, his followers recorded his sayings in a famous book called *The Analects*. Confucius's teachings greatly influenced the interpretation of Chinese history.

300 B.C.

Scholars at the Alexandrian Library began gathering copies of Homer's *Iliad* and *Odyssey*. Over many decades, they compared the copies and created "standard versions" of the stories. Today's scholars found a fragment of papyrus from around this time. It is the oldest written example of Homer's work.

200's B.C.

The Dead Sea Scrolls were written by several groups of people in ancient Jewish communities. In 1947, archaeologists discovered the scrolls in caves (below) near the Dead Sea, in the Middle East. The scrolls include fragments, or pieces, of many Biblical texts. The scrolls also included writings scholars had never seen before. Thousands of these fragments and over 900 manuscripts have been found at this site. They are among the oldest Hebrew texts in existence. The scrolls were written from the late 200's B.C. to A.D. 68, mostly on leather **parchment.**

Pisistratus (?-c. 527 B.C.) ruled Athens, Greece, during the mid-500's B.C. He may have started the city's first public library and encouraged poets and artists to work in Athens. In 300 B.C., Greek philosopher Aristotle (384 B.C.-322 B.C.) founded a famous library. He created the library as a place of research for the students at his school, The Lyceum, in Athens.

The largest of all the ancient libraries was located in Alexandria, Egypt. Alexander the Great (356 B.C.-323 B.C.) founded the library in the 330's B.C. This library borrowed important texts from other cities and made copies by hand on scrolls to keep in Alexandria. The Alexandrian Library became the finest collection of writing in the ancient world. It contained around 500,000 scrolls. But the library was destroyed in 200 A.D., and none of its collection remains.

Beginning around 200 B.C., parchment gradually replaced papyrus as the most commonly used writing material.

200's B.C.

c. 200 B.C.

The Septuagint, the Greek translation of the Hebrew Bible, began to be written down. According to legend, 72 Jewish scholars spent 72 days translating the text. But scholars think the Septuagint translation took over 200 years to complete. Christians call the Hebrew Bible the *Old Testament.*

Chapter 4

Developments in Writing Systems and Books

100 B.C.—c. A.D. 900's

Over the centuries, the ancient Romans made changes to the Greek **alphabet.** They added the letters *G*, *Y*, and *Z*. They also added some Etruscan characters, including *F* and *S*. The Romans changed most of the Greek letters into shapes with straight lines and curves. By around A.D. 1, their alphabet looked much like ours does today. But it did not include the letters *J*, *U*, or *W*.

37 B.C.

Emperor Augustus (63 B.C.-A.D. 14) ordered the construction of what may have been ancient Rome's first public library.

c. A.D. 1

By about A.D. 1, people in China had invented paper. To make the paper, they filtered water and plant *fibers* (woody stem material) through a fine screen. The fibers tangled together and dried to form one sheet—paper. At first, people used plant and tree fibers to make paper. Later, they formed fibers by pounding rags, rope, or nets into pulp.

A.D. 113

Trajan's Column is beautifully decorated with carved majuscules.

Much Roman writing was carved directly onto the walls of stone buildings and monuments. When carving into stone, people used capital, or upper-case, letters. Another name for upper-case letters is **majuscules.** (Lower-case letters were called **minuscules.**) A Roman column built in A.D. 113 has a beautiful example of carved majuscules. The writing on the column honors the emperor Trajan (A.D. 53?-A.D. 117). Today, Trajan's Column stands 100 feet (30 meters) high in Trajan's Forum in Rome, Italy.

Majuscule letters were not easy to write with pen and ink on **parchment.** Over time, people used a new lettering style that was easier to write with a pen. The new writing slanted to the right. It was called *cursive script.*

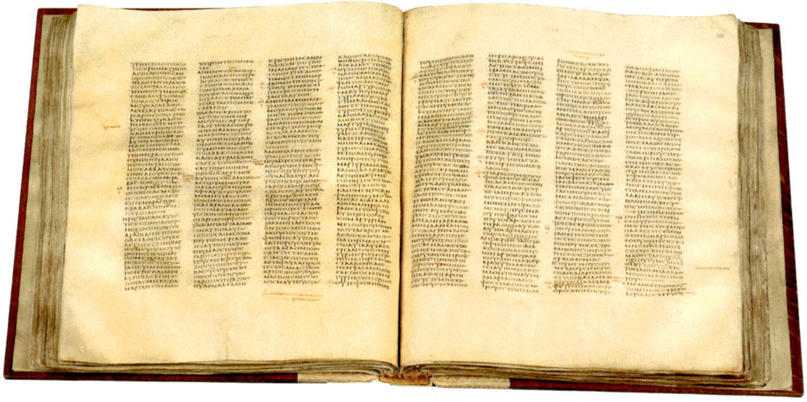

People invented a new way to bundle writing papers together. This bundle was called a **codex.** To make a codex, people grouped sheets of paper together and sewed them together on one side. Then to protect the pages, they bound, or attached, the sewed pages between two thin slices of wood. Before this time, people read on long scrolls. Only one side of the scroll paper was used. To read, people had to wind and rewind the long strips of the scroll. A codex was much smaller than a scroll. Both sides of the paper in the codex could be used. Readers could open the codex at any page. The codex developed into the types of books made today.

c. A.D. 1–A.D. 300

The New Testament, the second part of the Christian Bible, was written in Greek during this period.

c. A.D. 50–A.D. 125

Developments in Writing Systems and Books

100 B.C.—c. A.D. 900's

During the A.D. 200's, Germanic peoples of northern Europe developed a writing system called *runic.* The characters in the runic **alphabet** are known as **runes.** Early runes may have been used to write down charms and magic spells. Runes were carved onto slabs of stone or wood, or scratched onto coins and jewelry.

The Maya developed a writing system by A.D. 250. The Maya lived in what is now Mexico and Central America. Another civilization that lived west of the Maya, the Olmec, may have developed a writing system even earlier. Mayan writing was much like Egyptian **hieroglyphics**. It used more than 800 symbols. Some of these

Germanic people wrote with alphabet letters called *runes.* The first runes were mostly straight lines. Later runes had more complex shapes.

A.D. 200's

A.D. 200's

The Alexandrian Library was destroyed during a war for control of the Roman Empire.

The Maya had developed a writing system using many symbols.

c. A.D. 250

symbols stood for speech sounds. Others stood for words or ideas. Inscriptions of Mayan writing are found on standing stone slabs, sculptures, and pottery, as well as in a few surviving Mayan books.

In the Middle East, Arabs created a written form of their spoken language by the A.D. 600's. The Arabic alphabet is closely related to Aramaic. It has 28 symbols. They are written from right to left, or from the top of the page to the bottom.

Between the A.D. 600's and A.D. 900's, Arabic-speaking **Muslims** conquered North Africa and southwestern Asia. The Arabic language spread throughout these regions. People also began using versions of the Arabic alphabet to write other languages, including Persian and Turkish.

The earliest runic inscriptions in England date from the A.D. 400's. The Anglo-Saxons of England wrote their Old English script in runic until the A.D. 800's. After that, they began writing with the Latin alphabet.

A.D. 400's

A.D. 644–A.D. 656

The religion of Islam was founded in Arabia (now Saudi Arabia) by Muhammad (A.D. 570?-A.D. 632). After his death, the Muslim community wrote down his sayings in a book called the *Qur'ān.* Muslims consider this book sacred. The standard text of the Qur'ān was written between A.D. 644 and A.D. 656, during the reign of ruler Uthman ibn Affan (A.D. 575?-A.D. 656).

Developments in Writing Systems and Books

100 B.C.—c. A.D. 900's

During the **Middle Ages,** the Christian Church dominated learning in much of Europe. *Scribes* (writers) worked in churches and monasteries. They wrote books by hand on **parchment** pages. Much of their work involved making copies of Bibles, prayer books, and other religious works.

During the late A.D. 700's, scribes developed a new style of writing that made books easier to read. This style combined Roman **majuscule** (upper-case) letters with **minuscule** (lower-case) letters. Scribes started using punctuation marks. They also left spaces between words. This style of writing came to be known

A.D. 780's

The Carolingian Minuscule writing style was developed. It was named for Charlemagne (A.D. 742?-A.D. 814), a dominant ruler in Europe. Scribes at Charlemagne's palace school in Aachen, in present-day Germany, practiced the new lettering. The handwriting style later became the model for printing.

A.D. 700's

The Islamic Empire expanded into central Asia. As a result, the Chinese art of papermaking began to spread to the Middle East and other parts of the world.

mid-A.D. 700's–early A.D. 800's

The *Book of Kells* was created in a monastery, a religious community of men, in Kells, Ireland. It is one of the most beautiful examples of an illuminated manuscript.

as *Carolingian Minuscule.* Church scribes wanted to make their books look as beautiful as possible. They decorated many of the written pages with colorful designs and pictures. These works are known as *illuminated manuscripts*. Their rich colors, including gold and silver, seem to shine on the pages.

Around the same time in eastern Asia, a world-changing invention was taking shape. People there began carving letters, symbols, and pictures into wood blocks. Then they put ink on top of the raised images in the blocks. Finally, they pressed a sheet of paper onto the inked block. The ink "printed" impressions of the wood carvings onto the paper. By the A.D. 700's, this block printing method was used in China, Japan, and Korea.

A.D. 815

Caliph al-Ma'mun founded a great library in Baghdad (A.D. 786-A.D. 833), in what is now Iraq, called the House of Wisdom. Many scholars worked at the library. They translated ancient Greek and Roman texts into Arabic. They also wrote important new books about mathematics, science, and philosophy.

A.D. 868

The Chinese created the first known printed book. It was a text of the Buddhist religion called the *Diamond Sutra*. They used the block printing method.

c. A.D. 900's

Christian missionaries developed the Cyrillic writing system for the Slavic languages. These languages are spoken by people of eastern Europe and north and central Asia. The script is based on the 24-letter Greek alphabet. Slavic languages have more sounds than Greek. So, the missionaries gave the alphabet more letters. Modern Russian uses the Cyrillic alphabet, with 33 letters.

Chapter 5

The Rise of Printing

Mid-1000's—Late 1400's

The invention of block printing enabled people to make exact copies of books. However, it took a great deal of time to produce an entire book. The writing on each new page had to be carved into a block of wood. So, if a book had 100 pages, 100 blocks of wood were individually carved. Then, each block had to be put in order, inked, and pressed against paper. After this inking method, each completed page had to dry. Last, the dry pages were bound together.

1066

In the mid-1000's, the Normans, a group of conquerors who once lived in Scandinavia and then Normandy, France, moved into England. Normans spoke Old French. They had no letter for the *wuh* sound. This was a problem for Norman scribes because they needed to translate Old English words that used the sound. The scribes decided to push two v's together—*vv*. They called the letter *double v*. In English, the letter became known as *double u* or *w*.

Before this time, there was no dot over the lower-case letter *i*. Some scribes noticed that when an *i* was placed after an *l*, the two letters could be confused for an *h*. So, they started placing a dot over the *i* to help readers tell the two letters apart.

c. 1040

Chinese printer Bi Sheng (A.D. 990-1051) invented movable type printing in China. In movable type, letters, characters, and other symbols are carved or stamped on individual blocks. The blocks can be fairly readily arranged and rearranged on a plate to form words and sentences.

In the 1000's, a Chinese printer named Bi Sheng invented **movable type printing.** He made blocks with individual characters out of separate pieces of baked clay. In this way, he could arrange the characters in different patterns to produce the needed text. The characters could also be reused in later printings. But the Chinese writing system did not use an **alphabet.** It used thousands of different characters to represent words. Bi Sheng's invention was too difficult to use with so many different Chinese symbols. Most people continued using block printing.

In the 1300's, Europeans used block printing to make copies of such items as playing cards, religious images, and short books. The demand for books began to grow. Universities opened in European cities. There were more educated people—and more readers. Printers looked for easier and faster ways to make books.

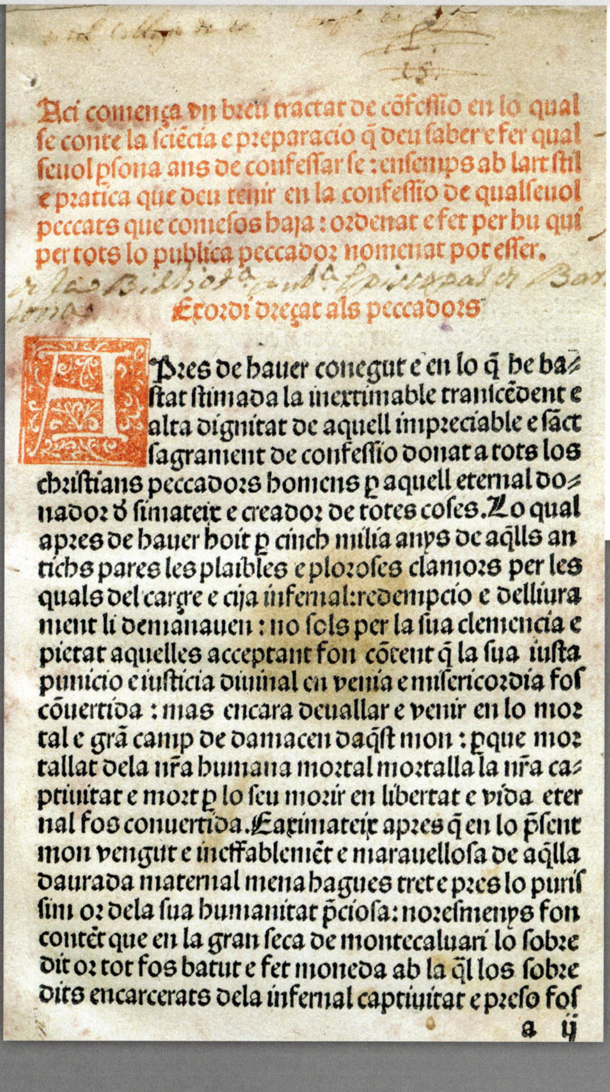

Aci comença vn breu tractat de cōfessio en lo qual
se conte la sciēcia e preparacio q̄ deu saber e fer qual
seuol psona ans de confessar se: ensemps ab lart stil
e pratica que deu tenir en la confessio de qualseuol
peccats que comesos haja: ordenat e fet per hu qui
per tots lo publica peccador nomenat pot esser.

Exordi dreçat als peccadors

Apres de hauer conegut e en lo q̄ he ba-
stat stimada la inextimable transcēdent e
alta dignitat de aquell impreciable e sāct
sagrament de confessio donat a tots los
christians peccadors homens p aquell eternal do-
nador d' simateix e creador de totes coses. Lo qual
apres de hauer hoit p cinch milia anys de aqlls an
tichs pares les plaibles e plorosos clamors per les
quals del cargre e cija infernal: redempcio e delliura
ment li demanauen: no sols per la sua clemencia e
pietat aquelles acceptant son cōsent q̄ la sua iusta
punicio e iusticia diuinal en venia e misericordia fos
cōuertida: mas encara deuallar e venir en lo mor
tal e grā camp de damacen daqst mon: pque mor
tallat dela nr̄a humana mortal mortalla la nr̄a ca-
ptiuitat e mort p lo seu morir en libertat e vida eter
nal fos conuertida. Eximateix apres q̄ en lo p̄sent
mon vengut e ineffablemēt e marauellosa de aqlla
daurada matemal mena hagues tret e pres lo puris
sim or dela sua humanitat p̄ciosa: no resmenys fon
contēt que en la gran seca de montecaluari lo sobre
dit or tot fos batut e fet moneda ab la ql los sobre
dits encarcerats dela infernal captiuitat e preso fos
a ij

1100's

The Carolingian Minuscule handwriting style gradually changed into a style known as *blackletter,* or *gothic*. Blackletter developed because of a growing demand for books from universities. This style, which developed over many years, was narrower and denser. More words could fit on a page, which meant less **parchment** was used. Blackletter took less time and effort to produce than Carolingian.

1200's

In Europe, paper made of cotton and linen began to replace parchment. Paper was not as strong as parchment, but was far less expensive to make.

1300's

People in Korea invented a technique of movable type printing using metal characters. But Korean writing, like Chinese, used far more symbols than an alphabet. Like Bi Sheng's earlier clay movable type, the Koreans' invention was not widely used.

The Rise of Printing

Mid-1000's—Late 1400's

In the mid-1400's, a German inventor named Johannes Gutenberg made a **movable type printing** press using metal characters. The Koreans and Chinese invented a similar technology centuries earlier. But these earlier inventors were missing a key ingredient: an **alphabet.** The Chinese and Koreans used hundreds of symbols for writing—too many to easily arrange for printing. But the Latin alphabet, with just a handful of letters, worked perfectly.

In his machine, Gutenberg set letters or symbols one by one into wooden frames to form pages. He placed the frame on the flat bed of a press. Then he applied ink

Printer Johannes Gutenberg (1395?-1468?) began his most famous work, known as the *Gutenberg Bible*. He and his team printed around 150 copies of the book, of which 21 complete copies still exist today. The Bible took several months of work to print. Six men set the Latin type for each page. Scholars call it the *42-line Bible* because most of the pages have 42 lines of type in each column. Colorful designs decorate its pages.

Mid-1400's

1469

German printer Johannes de Spira set up the first printing press in Venice, Italy. The city soon became a center for printing and the book trade.

1470

French printer Nicolas Jenson (1404-1480) designed a **typeface,** or **font,** called Venetian Oldstyle. It was a roman typeface, meaning the letter strokes ended in thin lines called *serifs*. Most roman typefaces today are based on his design.

on top of the metal characters and pressed paper onto them. With Gutenberg's invention, printers could copy around 300 pages a day. Scribes making copies of books by hand could not match the speed of the printing press.

Soon, people set up print shops in cities across Germany, France, Italy, and Spain. The books printed between 1450 and 1500 are known as *incunabula*, from the Latin word for *cradle* (*incunabulum*), because they were produced during the infancy of printing. Printers of incunabula were strongly influenced by handwritten manuscripts from the **Middle Ages.** They used large **type** that resembled handwritten letters on the printing press. They also printed books on expensive, handmade paper or **parchment.** Individual pages were often decorated or illustrated by hand.

Englishman William Caxton (1422?-1492) produced the first printed book in the English language called *Recuyell of the Historyes of Troye*. *Recuyell* means a grouping. Caxton's spellings may look strange, but it would be years before English spelling became *standardized* (the same everywhere). Later, Caxton established the first printing press in England. His shop printed *The Canterbury Tales* (below) by English poet Geoffrey Chaucer (1340?-1400).

1473

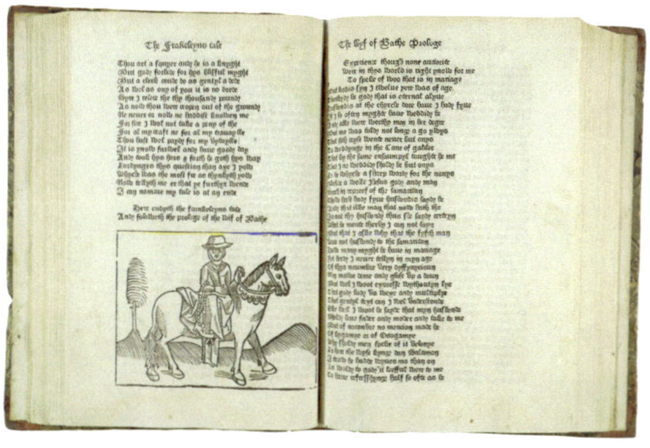

1490's

Venetian printer Aldus Manutius (1449-1515) established the Aldine Press in Venice. Manutius became famous for his beautiful editions of classic Greek and Roman works. His books were small and inexpensive. Manutius also invented **italic** type. Italic words are slanted, *like this*, to stand out from the rest of the text.

Chapter 6

The Influence of Printing

Early 1500's—Late 1700's

By 1500, over a thousand print shops had opened in Europe. Millions of books had been printed at low cost. As a result, more people could afford to buy books than ever before. With the printing press, new knowledge spread quickly. More people learned how to read.

Social changes spread with the great variety of printed books. The **Renaissance** (meaning *rebirth*) was a period from about 1300 to the 1600's. The Renaissance

1517

According to tradition, German monk Martin Luther (1483-1546) posted his Ninety-Five Theses on the door of Wittenberg Castle Church in Germany. His theses were statements against certain practices of the Roman Catholic Church. Luther believed the Catholics were ignoring the text of the Bible. Earlier Europeans relied on Catholic scribes and clergy to understand the Bible because it was only available in Latin. But now many Europeans could read the Bible themselves because it was printed in their own language. This movement became known as the Reformation.

1529

French printer Geoffroy Tory (1480-1533) made important advances in printing. He helped popularize roman **type.** In his book *Champfleury*, printed in 1529, he introduced accent marks, the apostrophe, and simple punctuation marks. Similarly, printer Simon de Colines (1480-1546) pioneered the use of **italic** type in France.

1539

Italian printer Juan Pablos (Giovanni Paoli, 1500?-1560?) set up a print shop in Mexico City. It was the first print shop in North America.

began as Italians rediscovered the art and ideas of ancient Greece and Rome. More people became interested in science, art, literature, and history. Printing helped spread these ideas quickly throughout Europe. In the 1500's, a movement called the **Reformation** challenged the authority of the Roman Catholic Church. Printed books helped to spread this movement's ideas. Within decades, nearly half of Europe had abandoned Roman Catholicism to become Protestant Christians.

Books themselves also changed. Early printed books looked similar to illuminated manuscripts. But during the 1500's, printed books became smaller. Their **typeface** letters became much easier to read. Many contained block-printed illustrations. By the late 1500's, most books had page numbers, a table of contents, and an index.

Pope Paul IV (1476-1559), the leader of the Roman Catholic Church, **published** the first Index of Forbidden Books in 1559. (A later edition, from 1570, is shown right.) The pope said Catholics were not allowed to read any book on the *Index* (list). The books were censored in this way because the Church considered them harmful to faith and morals. Censorship means controlling, changing, or destroying written works, works of art, and other expressions of thought and creativity. But censoring written material became much harder in the age of printing. The Church maintained the Index of Forbidden Books until 1966.

PHILIPPI II.
REGIS CATHOLICI
EDICTVM
De Librorum prohibitorum Catalogo obſeruando.

ANTVERPIAE,
Ex officina Chriſtophori Plantini.
M. D. LXX.

1559

The Influence of Printing

Early 1500's—Late 1700's

During the 1600's, the number of readers in Europe continued to grow. Printers **published** many types of books. New books included small, cheap works meant for all people to read, not just scholars. The printing press also reached the colonies in North America. Printed materials were shared among continents through merchant and passenger ships. With printed texts, people were able to more easily share knowledge, books, and news over longer distances.

During the 1600's, a new form of fiction developed, later called the *novel.* Fiction is a story that is not fact. Unlike **epic** poems and other literature from the **Middle**

1602

English statesman Sir Thomas Bodley (1545-1613) reopened an earlier library at the University of Oxford. He donated books, manuscripts, and money, and encouraged others to donate. It was named the Bodleian Library in his honor. Today, this is the second largest library in the United Kingdom.

1605–1615

One of the first published novels was *Don Quixote* by Spanish author Miguel de Cervantes (1547-1616). Cervantes published it in two parts, in 1605 and 1615. The book is about the adventures of a nobleman, Don Quixote, who mistakenly believes himself to be a knight performing heroic deeds. This mistake results in many comic episodes.

1638

Massachusetts clergyman John Harvard (1607-1638) founded the Harvard University Library. It remains the oldest library in the United States and the world's largest library system.

Ages, novels were not usually about great heroes. The language was not poetic. Rather, the characters and settings tended to be closer to everyday life.

During this time, the first regularly published, or printed, newspapers appeared. Pamphlets were another important kind of publication. Pamphlets were short, cheap printed works. They usually made an argument about religion or politics. Governments often tried to censor newspapers and pamphlets.

The expansion of printing and knowledge also dramatically increased the number of libraries in Europe. Many important libraries were founded in the 1600's, especially at universities.

1639

English locksmith Stephen Daye (1594?-1668) and his son Matthew set up the first printing press in Cambridge, Massachusetts. In 1640, the Dayes produced the first book known to have been printed in the English colonies of America The book, titled the *Bay Psalm Book*, is a collection of Bible *hymns* (songs) translated into English.

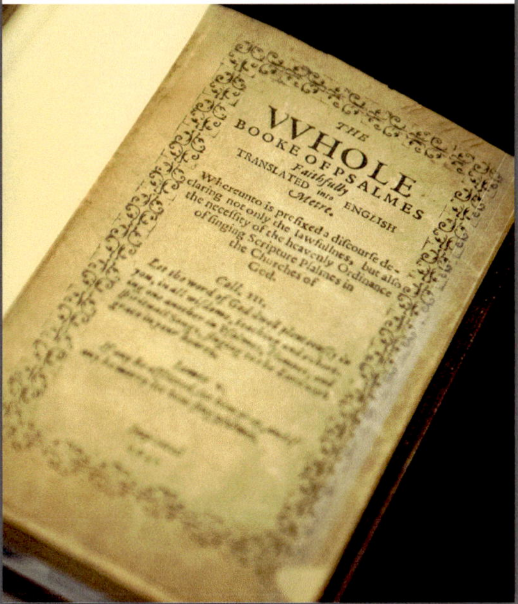
THE VVHOLE BOOKE OF PSALMES Faithfully TRANSLATED into ENGLISH Metre.

Whereunto is prefixed a discourse declaring not only the lawfullnes, but also the necessity of the heavenly Ordinance of singing Scripture Psalmes in the Churches of God.

1643

The Licensing Order of 1643 was a law passed by the Parliament of England to control what material printers could publish. It allowed the government to destroy any books it found offensive. The law also gave power to arrest and imprison authors and printers.

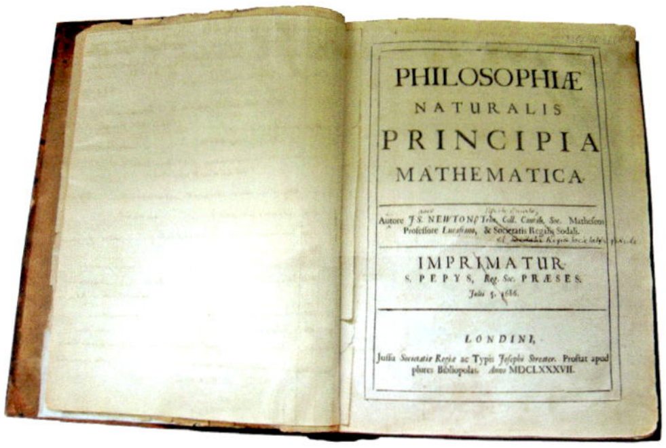
PHILOSOPHIÆ NATURALIS PRINCIPIA MATHEMATICA

IMPRIMATUR S. PEPYS, Reg. Soc. PRÆSES.

LONDINI,

English mathematician Sir Isaac Newton (1642-1727) published *Philosophiae naturalis principia mathematica (Mathematical Principles of Natural Philosophy)*. Newton's work explained how all of nature obeyed mathematical laws of motion. His book laid much of the foundation for modern science and industry. It also greatly influenced philosophers of the Enlightenment.

1687

The Influence of Printing

Early 1500's—Late 1700's

Printing helped spread the ideas of a movement called the *Enlightenment.* This movement began in the 1600's and continued until the late 1700's. Enlightenment philosophers believed truth could be discovered only through reason and science. They thought that the advancement of knowledge was the best way to improve humanity. Enlightenment scholars gathered, organized, and **published** this knowledge in printed books. Printing allowed information to spread quickly and accurately. Scholars working in different parts of Europe could publish their work and share it with each other. Publishing helped advance knowledge and ideas.

1690

Benjamin Harris (1660?-1720) of Boston founded the first newspaper in the English colonies of America. The colonial government shut it down after just one issue.

1731

American colonist and statesman Benjamin Franklin (1706-1790) helped establish the Library Company of Philadelphia. It was the first subscription library in America. People paid dues to become members of the library. The money was used to buy books. Members could then use the library books. The company was a success, encouraging many other subscription libraries to open.

1751

Two French authors, Denis Diderot (1713-1784) and Jean d'Alembert (1717-1783), began publishing a 28-volume encyclopedia. Their work, completed in 1772, was not the first encyclopedia in history. But, it was the most important reference work of the Enlightenment. Reference works organize knowledge and collect it in one place—a major goal of the Enlightenment.

In the 1700's, schoolchildren in Europe and the United States were taught an elegant new style of cursive handwriting. This writing was known as *copperplate* because the workbooks from which students learned this style were printed on copper plate printing presses.

From an early age, more and more people were learning to read and write—increasing the demand for printed books. By the late 1700's, however, the printing process had not changed very much since the days of Gutenberg. It remained a time-consuming process. Printers could not produce enough books to keep up with demand. Soon, though, a new revolution would make it easier to print books than ever before.

1752

Canadian printer John Bushell (1715-1761?) began publishing the *Halifax Gazette*, the first newspaper in what is now the nation of Canada.

1791

The United States Bill of Rights, which states the first 10 amendments to the Constitution, went into effect. The First Amendment guarantees freedom of the press. Freedom of the press is the right of a printer or publisher to publish facts, ideas, and opinions without interference from the government or other groups. Though there are some limits in place, democratic countries still grant freedom of the press to encourage the exchange of ideas and to limit the power of the government.

1798

German printer Alois Senefelder (1771-1834) accidentally invented a new printing process called **lithography.** While preparing to carve into a stone slab, he wrote on the slab with a wax crayon. He found that instead of carving the stone, the wax marks could be inked and the image printed on paper. Lithography is successful because oil (in the crayon or in ink) and water (on the blank areas of the stone) do not mix.

Chapter 7

Mass-Produced Texts

Early 1800's—Early 1960's

During the late 1700's and 1800's, a series of inventions revolutionized book manufacturing. The inventions were part of the rapid development of industry known as the *Industrial Revolution.* It was a time of great change in society and technology. People started using steam-powered machines, including printing presses. Factories could produce many goods quickly and inexpensively. Machines made paper and bound books. These advances made possible the mass

1811

German printers Friedrich Koenig (1774-1833) and Andreas Bauer (1783-1860) invented a steam-powered cylinder press. This machine used a rotating cylinder, or tube, that pressed the paper against a flat bed of **type.** *The Times*, a London newspaper, began using the press in 1814. It could print 1,100 sheets of paper per hour.

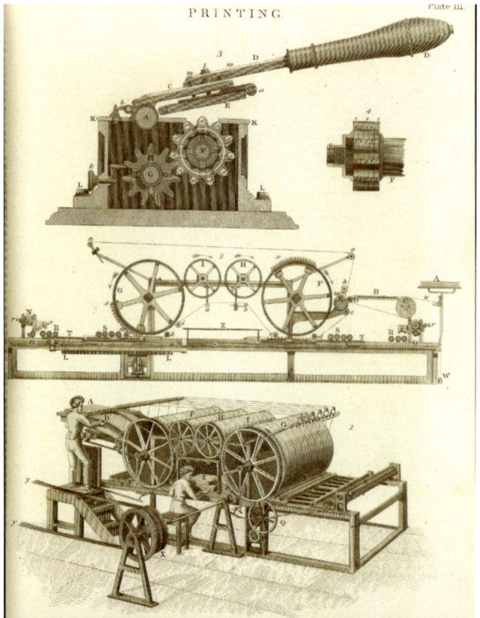

1829

French educator Louis Braille (1809-1852), who was blinded in a childhood accident, published the braille system of writing and printing for the blind. Braille is a code of small, raised dots on paper that can be read by touch. His dot system was based on a "cell" of six dots. From the 63 possible arrangements of the dots, Braille created an **alphabet,** punctuation marks, numerals, and, later, a system for writing music. His code later won universal acceptance for all written languages.

production of newspapers and books. Mass production helped literacy spread to the working classes. Cheap books with paper covers, called *paperbacks*, became popular around 1870. Printing became one of the most important means of **mass communication.**

The business of book manufacturing also changed in the 1800's. Instead of one company printing, **publishing,** and selling its works, a new kind of business emerged—the publisher. A publisher develops the content, or words, in a book or newspaper. Then, the publisher hires a printing company to print and bind the work. The publisher then sells the books. Bookshops and public lending libraries opened up in many towns and cities. Many people became professional writers, working for newspapers or publishing popular books.

1833

One of the first public libraries in the United States opened in Peterborough, New Hampshire. Unlike earlier subscription libraries, people could use the library for free. Taxes paid for the library's books and services.

1846

Richard Hoe (1812-1886), an American manufacturer of printing presses, invented the rotary press. Instead of having a flat bed of type, Hoe attached type to a revolving cylinder, or tube. Another cylinder pressed paper against the inked type. Hoe's presses could print 8,000 sheets of paper per hour. Later versions of his machine could print 20,000 sheets per hour.

1865

American machine inventor William Bullock (1813-1867) created a press that used a giant roll of paper. This type of machine is called a *web-fed press.* Individual pages are cut from the roll after printing.

Mass-Produced Texts

Early 1800's—Early 1960's

One of the problems of widespread printing was that anyone could print any book without its author's permission. Copyright is a collection of rights granted to creators of original works. The Berne Convention for the Protection of Literary and Artistic Works of 1866 was the first major international copyright agreement. A version of the convention's rules is still used today.

Meanwhile, during the late 1800's and 1900's, the printing industry continued to advance. New technology improved the quality and reduced the cost of printing. Offset **lithographic** printing was one major advance. With this method, a press

1884

German-born inventor Ottmar Mergenthaler (1854-1899) created the Linotype machine. Since Gutenberg's day, press workers assembled metal characters one by one by hand in a simple tool called a *composing stick.* With the Linotype, they could now enter text on a keyboard. Then, the machine automatically assembled the text into lines of **type.**

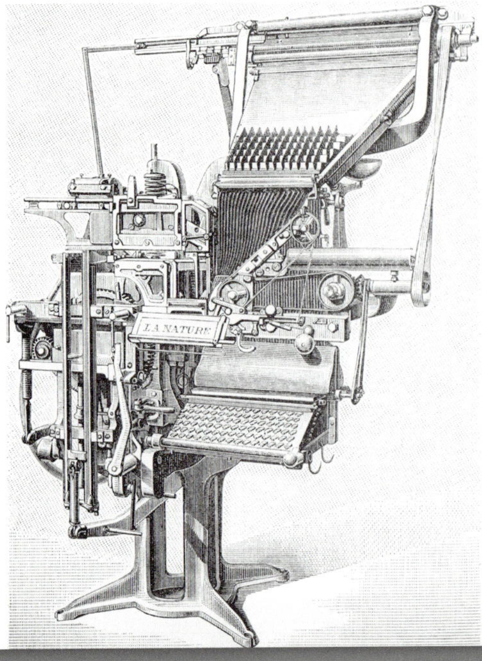

1886

Copyright rules were established to protect authors' rights to their works.

c. 1905

In the 1800's, German printer Alois Senefelder's lithographic process became a practical printing method. Around 1905, American papermaker and printer Ira Rubel (1860-1908) improved this method. Rubel accidentally transferred an inked image onto a rubber-covered cylinder. When he transferred the image from the rubber onto paper, he noticed it was much sharper. This method is called *offset lithographic printing*. Soon, offset printing became widespread.

transfers ink to a rubber cylinder. The cylinder, in turn, transfers the ink to the page. Such images are much sharper than those printed directly from a press.

Later, publishers developed a four-color printing process. With different combinations of four inks, printers could create many colors. The process is used to produce inexpensive illustrated books and magazines with color. Eventually, new machines could print and bind books in a single operation. Many of these types of machines are still used today.

Handwriting also changed during the 1900's. Schoolchildren in the United States and United Kingdom were taught simpler, clearer styles of writing. Cursive writing was treated as a practical skill rather than an art.

1930's

Paperback books rose in popularity.

1960's

Phototypesetting began replacing the Linotype machine. In phototypesetting, **type** is set using photography. By shining light through a photograph of a character, an image of that character could be made on a material much like camera film. The image could then be transferred to a printing plate. This method was much more flexible than Linotype. For example, the size of letters and line spacing could easily be changed.

Early 1960's

Publishers began using special computers to speed up production of braille books. Text is typed into a computer that automatically translates it into braille. The computer then transfers the raised braille figures onto paper or onto metal plates for use in a press.

Chapter 8

The Written Word Today

Mid-1980's—Today

Since the late 1900's and early 2000's, computers have transformed the way books are written and **published.** The process began with personal computers, which became popular in the late 1980's. People could use desktop publishing computer programs to write, illustrate, and design their own original works for publication.

Computers did not just make printed works easier to make. People could also

1984

American computer manufacturer Apple Computer, Inc. introduced its Macintosh® personal computer. The Macintosh was useful for desktop publishing. It could display text and images on its screen just as they would appear on a printed page. People could easily create their own printed works from the convenience of their desk.

1991

British computer scientist Tim Berners-Lee (1955-) developed the World Wide Web. He invented hypertext—words or images that link to web pages.

1999

Blogger™ and LiveJournal™, two popular public blogging services, launched.

Early 2000's

Print-on-demand technology became popular. Publishers and self-published authors could print only as many copies of a work as they needed—even a single copy.

read on computer screens—no paper needed. Since the 1990's, vast amounts of written material have been created, designed, and posted on the Internet—without ever appearing in printed form. Websites have become a major way people read and share news, knowledge, and ideas. With **hypertext**—linked words and images—people can jump between websites as easily as turning a book's page. *Blogs* (short for *web logs*) enable people to easily post their own writing on websites.

People continue to read books, but many now appear in electronic form. Such **e-books** became popular in the 2000's. E-books are purchased and viewed on an e-reader or another computerized device with an Internet connection. But for many readers, printed books will always have a place on their bookshelves.

2007

The online retailer Amazon.com® launched its popular e-book reader, the Kindle™. Such devices also function like handheld libraries or bookstores. An e-reader can store hundreds of books. Users can usually buy and download books from the Internet straight onto their device. Other small computers, such as smartphones and tablets, often include e-reader *apps* (programs). These apps have similar functions.

2011

In 2011, Amazon.com® sold more e-books than print books.

2012

December 31: *Newsweek*, an internationally read news magazine, published its last print edition. After 79 years of print, *Newsweek* became an all-digital product.

Glossary

alphabet a writing system that uses symbols called *letters.* Each letter stands for a certain speech sound of a language.

codex the modern form of a book: individual pages bound together along one side and placed within a cover.

cuneiform a system of writing made up of wedge-shaped characters.

e-book an electronic version of a printed book, which can be read on a computer, e-reader, or other device.

epic a long poem, typically one narrating the adventures of heroic figures.

hieroglyphics a form of writing in which picture symbols represent ideas, words, and sounds.

hypertext a computer language used to create Internet websites.

italic a sloping typeface used to make certain words stand out from the text.

lithography the process of printing from a treated flat surface. The flat surface holds ink only where needed for printing.

majuscule large capital lettering in which all letters are the same height; upper-case letters.

mass communication any form of communication (such as newspapers, radio, or television) that reaches large numbers of people.

Middle Ages the period in European history between ancient and modern times, from about the A.D. 400's through about the 1400's. The end date depends on the region of Europe considered.

minuscule small lettering in which all letters are the same height; lower-case letters.

movable type printing a system of printing in which letters, characters, and other symbols are carved or stamped on individual blocks. The blocks can be reused and rearranged in any combination.

Muslim a person who follows the religion of Islam.

papyrus a paperlike material made from the stems of plants.

parchment a writing surface made from animal skins, used in scrolls and in early books.

pictogram a picture sign that stands for a word, phrase, or idea.

publish to prepare a written work for distribution to the public.

Reformation a movement in the 1500's that challenged the Roman Catholic Church, resulting in the establishment of Protestant Christian churches.

Renaissance a great cultural movement that began in Italy during the early 1300's.

runes letters of an ancient Germanic alphabet.

type characters or letters that are printed on paper or shown on a screen.

typeface a particular design of type; also called **font.**

Find Out More

Books

The Age of the Book by Renzo Rossi (Benchmark, 2009)

Communication in the Ancient World by Hazel Richardson (Crabtree, 2012)

The Epic of Gilgamesh retold by Geraldine McCaughrean (Eerdmans Books for Young Readers, 2003)

From the Good Mountain: How Gutenberg Changed the World by James Rumford (Roaring Brook Press, 2012)

Ox, House, Stick: The History of Our Alphabet by Don Robb (Charlesbridge, 2007)

The Story of Writing by Carol Donoughue (Firefly Books, 2007)

You Wouldn't Want to Live Without Books! by Alex Woolf (Franklin Watts, 2015)

You Wouldn't Want to Live Without Writing! by Roger Canavan (Franklin Watts, 2016)

Websites

BBC History – The Decipherment of Hieroglyphs
http://www.bbc.co.uk/history/ancient/egyptians/decipherment_01.shtml
Learn how to decipher Egyptian hieroglyphs and the Rosetta Stone using historical photos.

The British Museum – Explore / Writing
http://www.britishmuseum.org/explore/themes/writing/historic_writing.aspx
View early writing systems etched on ancient *artifacts* (items or tools made by humans) while learning about the artifacts' historical importance.

The British Museum – Mesopotamia: Writing
http://www.mesopotamia.co.uk/writing/home_set.html
Click on ancient stone carvings to learn more about scribes and the development of the writing system.

Harry Ransom Center – Printing Yesterday and Today
http://www.hrc.utexas.edu/educator/modules/gutenberg/books/printing/
See historical illustrations, artifacts, and photographs of printing technology from Gutenberg's first machine to today's press.

International Printing Museum – Collection
http://www.printmuseum.org/museum/collection/
Take an in-depth look at a collection of historic printing presses.

Museum of the American Printing House for the Blind – Callahan Gallery
http://www.aph.org/museum/programs/main-gallery/
Virtually tour a museum dedicated to understanding of how people with visual impairments experience the world.

NOVA – Origins of the Written Bible
http://www.pbs.org/wgbh/nova/ancient/origins-written-bible.html
Read an informative essay that traces the origins of the written Bible.

Index

Seeing Yourself in God's Image:
Overcoming Anorexia and Bulimia

Facilitator's Guide

By Martha Homme, M.A., L.P.

Communications should be addressed to:
Turning Point Ministries, Inc.
P. O. Box 22127
Chattanooga, TN 37422-2127

ISBN 1-58119-037-9

Turning Point®

Cover Design: Graphic Advertising
Layout: Louise Lee

About the Author

Martha Homme, M.A., L.P., completed her undergraduate degree in Foods and Nutrition at the University of North Carolina in Greensboro. She holds an M.A. in Education from the University of Minnesota and an M.A. in Counseling from the Alfred Adler Institute.

Martha's involvement with eating disorder counseling grew out of personal survival of an adolescent eating disorder. Years later she is still convinced that Jesus is the only answer to freedom from bondage to the lies of our sociocultural and family systems. These lies lead to the elevation of food to the status of a false god which robs an individual of knowledge of the truth that unconditional love and acceptance are found only when our identity is in Christ.

In addition to her private practice, Martha is an Assessment and Referral Counselor and Marriage Preparation Instructor for Crystal Evangelical Free Church in New Hope, Minnesota. She also developed and facilitates the support group, *Weigh Out: Understanding and Overcoming Anorexia and Bulimia.*

Seeing Yourself in God's Image:
Overcoming Anorexia and Bulimia

Contents

Preface

Seeing Yourself in God's Image

The primary purpose of food is to satisfy physical hunger. God created all food to be good. He does not, however, intend that food nor our attitude toward it become our God. Neither is He pleased with us when we place inappropriate focus on our body image making it, in essence, an idol. *I am the LORD your God, who brought you out of Egypt, out of the land of slavery. You shall have no other gods before me. You shall not make for yourself an idol in the form of anything in heaven above or on the earth beneath or in the waters below* (Deuteronomy 5:6-8).

This material provides a challenging journey into freedom from bondage to two eating disorders: ***anorexia and bulimia***

Chaotic eating occurs when we let eating (or not eating) dominate our lives and when we worry more about our physical shape than we do about our spiritual and emotional worth and well-being. The ABCs of *chaotic eating* are **A**—anorexia, **B**—bulimia, and **C**—compulsive overeating. This material provides a challenging journey into freedom from bondage to two eating disorders: anorexia and bulimia. (The focus of this support group guide is anorexia and bulimia since they tend to be more identified as *eating disorders.* The principles of bondage to food apply to compulsive overeating; hence, it should not be ignored as an eating disorder.)

Ten major emotional and perceptual characteristics contribute to the development of *anorexia or bulimia:*

- Distorted Body Image and Denial
- Irrational Beliefs and Distorted Thinking
- Perfectionism
- Low Self-Esteem
- Depression
- Control
- Dependency
- Distorted Sexual Identity
- Dysfunctional Family System
- Sociocultural Influence

The eating disordered behaviors (restricting, binging, purging, etc.) are a cover for these underlying problems. Medical management of eating disordered behaviors is critical to restoring physical well-being. Psychological, emotional, and spiritual management of the eating disordered personality distortions are essential to restoration of God's plan for each of His creation: significance, self-worth, safety/security, and belongingness. (Although referral to a medical doctor or a Christian psychologist, psychiatrist, and/or dietitian is imperative for the physical, emotional, and psychological management of an eating disorder, collaborative spiritual management and accountability are important roles of a Christian support group.)

Getting Started

Group Size
We suggest that each *Seeing Yourself in God's Image* group have two group leaders (facilitators) and a maximum of twelve participants. Having more than twelve may prevent some from being a part of much-needed discussion.

Preparation Time
The facilitator's material is written in an almost word-for-word dialogue. However, it is hoped that as you come to know and understand the concepts presented, you will be able to "personalize" each session to fit your own style better. Highlight the points you want to emphasize and make notes for yourself.

Your group is unique—so adapt questions to their needs and situations. Be sensitive to each person who is in your group.

Keep in mind that the answers provided for the discussion questions are there only as a tool to assist you and may not be the only "right" answers to the questions being asked.

Become thoroughly familiar with the four elements of each session:

- Introduction
- Self-Awareness
- Spiritual Awareness
- Application

You will find more detail about these on the following pages.

The facilitators should meet prior to each session to pray and make final plans. They should also meet briefly after each session to discuss what happened during the meeting and go over any follow-up that may be needed.

***Seeing Yourself in God's Image* Group Workbooks**
Before Session 1, the *Seeing Yourself in God's Image* group workbook should be distributed to each group member. Facilitators should be thoroughly familiar with the workbook before the first meeting.

During the orientation, encourage group members to complete the appropriate assignments prior to each group meeting. Through the readings and other exercises in the workbook, group members can come to each session better prepared for meaningful discussion.

Suggested Group Format

The group format for each session consists of four elements: Introduction, Self-Awareness, Spiritual Awareness, and Application. There is a reason for each phase. The facilitators should always plan each session with this format in mind.

Part I Introduction
(10 minutes)
Begin with prayer. The facilitator may pray or may ask one of the group members to lead in prayer. After the prayer, a sharing question helps put the group at ease and makes the members more comfortable in being a part of the discussion. The lead facilitator should respond to the sharing question first, followed by the co-facilitator. This helps the group members to feel safer in participating in the exercise. After the facilitators have shared, the group members will share one after another around the circle. Always remind group members they are not expected to share if they do not wish to do so. The rule is that everyone works within his or her comfort level and is welcome to pass.

This is not the time for detailed conversation, so ask the members of the group to keep their comments brief. If a person is obviously in pain during the exercise, the facilitator should interrupt the sharing and pray for the person in pain. After prayer, the exercise may resume.

Part II Self-Awareness
(20-25 minutes)
After the sharing question, the facilitator will lead the group into the Self-Awareness phase. Self-Awareness is a time to discuss the practical issues involved in *Seeing Yourself in God's Image.* It is important to stay on the subject matter. This is a time to focus on needs and healing, not to have a "martyr" or "pity party."

It is suggested in Self-Awareness that the facilitators ask the group members to share as they wish rather than going around the circle as in the introduction phase. This is because people are at various comfort levels, and they should not feel pressured to self-disclose if they are uncomfortable. As the group continues to meet, members will feel more and more comfortable in being a part of the discussion.

Remember, prayer is always in order. If a group member is hurting during this phase, stop and pray. One of the facilitators may lead in prayer or ask another group member to pray. This says to the group members that each one is important and that you care about each individual.

Part III Spiritual Awareness
(20-25 minutes)
After the Self-Awareness phase, the facilitator will lead the group into the bible study time. Having briefly explained the topic, the facilitator should assign scriptures listed in the Facilitator's Guide to group members. When each Scripture is called by the facilitator, the group member should read the verse(s). After the verses are read, give time for discussion.

Part IV Application
(20 minutes)
This part is actually a continuation of Part III. Ask for volunteers to share their reflections on the questions. The facilitators should emphasize the importance of the group members' applying biblical principles to their lives. Help begins with right thinking. The Bible says, "Be transformed by the renewing of your mind" (Romans 12:2). Obedience to the Word should follow with right behavior. Right feelings will follow right thinking and right behavior.

Session 1 Eating Disorders: An Overview

Introduction

Allow 10 Minutes

Opening Prayer

Take a few moments to thank God for each person in the group. Express thanks for each group member's desire to be restored to physical, emotional, and spiritual health.

Welcome

The purpose of this exercise is to help group members move toward being more comfortable sharing with the group. Initially sharing names only, followed by the facilitators' orientation (foundation building and group goals), encourages the members to focus their more detailed introductions on eating disordered related information about themselves.

Welcome to our first session of *Seeing Yourself in God's Image.* Let's begin by sharing our names with one another. Shortly, after I lay a brief foundation, share the goals for our group, and review group ground rules, I'll ask each of you to share why you joined the group. My name is ________________, and my co-facilitator is ______________________.

Foundation building — Genesis 1:26 reminds us that we are created in the image of God. God created each of us to have *identity.* His positive *identity plan* consists of both physical and spiritual well-being. It includes access to significance, self-worth, safety/security, and belongingness. Unfortunately, the impact of the fall, even for the Christian, causes a vulnerability toward the dominant negative emotional and spiritual effects of rejection, shame, guilt, hopelessness, and powerlessness.

Instead of claiming our identity in Christ, we too often seek significance, self-worth, safety/security, and belongingness in the wrong places. Thinness, performance, and control do not equal significance and wholeness. When we fail to recognize that we are unconditionally loved and regarded by our heavenly Father, we set ourselves up for rejection, shame, guilt, hopelessness, and powerlessness. The positive attributes of our position in Christ are replaced by the eating disordered distortions with their need to *perform, please,* or *control.*

Goals of the group — The goals of *Seeing Yourself in God's Image* include providing an opportunity for:

1. Increased understanding of what an eating disorder is and how it affects the physical, emotional, psychological, and spiritual well-being of individuals and their relationships at home, work, and elsewhere.
2. Identification of ten major factors which contribute to the emotional and perceptual makeup of the eating disordered *personality.*
3. Identification of the *lies we believe* (cognitive distortions) which trigger eating disordered behaviors.

4. Practice using tools designed to address and reframe eating disordered behaviors and beliefs cognitively, emotionally, psychologically, physically, and spiritually using scripture, prayer, mutual support, and bible-based self-knowledge.
5. Increased understanding of the relationship between eating disordered behavior and spiritual warfare.

GROUP GROUND RULES

Everyone participates.
Everyone has the right to pass.
We share mutual respect.
Confidentiality is strictly honored (what is said here, stays here).

Now let's continue our introductions by sharing briefly what brings us to *Seeing Yourself in God's Image.* I'll begin by giving you a snapshot of my background. (Keep in mind that when we share in group, everyone is encouraged to share, but *passing* is always an option.)

Personal introductions.

Self-Awareness

Allow 20–25 Minutes

Eating, a normal life function, becomes an eating disorder when the primary need it satisfies is psychological, not physical. Eating behaviors have become a vehicle for the expression of problems in personal identity and in relationships with others. An eating disorder is not merely a problem with food or weight. It is an attempt to use control to solve unseen emotional conflicts or difficulties that in fact have little to do with either food or weight. An eating disorder is not ever simply a matter of self-control. Stronger will-power or healthier eating habits are not the missing ingredients that will make the problem disappear.

An eating disorder is someone's attempt to feel better about herself (or himself*) or to help her function in a world that feels intimidating. The destructiveness of eating disordered behaviors (binging, purging, restricting, etc.) is a by-product of the problem, not an intent.

An eating disorder is a perceived external solution to inner turmoil. The focus on body size is an attempt to convert a worry about something inside oneself to something outside oneself. For example, if the concern, "Am I good enough?" becomes "Am I thin enough?" the sufferer creates an external and measurable scale of her self-worth that offers a less painful and more comprehensible way to cope.

* The feminine pronoun is used in the text; however, males are also subject to eating disorders and the percentages are gradually increasing.

By focusing on weight as the source of all discomfort, she leaves untouched the tumultuous and confusing feelings inside of her. An eating disorder is a form of substance abuse relying on an external substance to alleviate internal distress. When used for emotional purposes, food functions similarly to drugs or alcohol. It provides escape. Spiritually speaking, it also provides bondage to disobedience. (This will be discussed more in the *Spiritual Awareness* portion of this session.)

Signs and Symptoms of Eating Disorders

The presence of an eating disorder is not always obvious. The following clues may indicate that you or someone you care about may have an eating disorder:

- Preoccupation with dieting, food, weight, calories, and body size.
- Unexplained weight loss.
- Frequent gazing at mirrors.
- Discomfort when eating in the company of others. Isolated eating.
- Marked changes in habits, moods, or personality.
- Hyperactivity.
  Preoccupation with exercise.
  Exercising beyond exhaustion and physical limitations.
- Inability to concentrate.
  Restlessness.
  Distractibility.
  Unexplained drop in grades.
- Difficulty sleeping. Changes in sleeping patterns.
- Ritualistic behavior, especially in connection with food.
- Intestinal disturbances and headaches.
- Loss of or change in menstruation.
- Problems with interpersonal relationships. Withdrawal from friends or society in general.

Can you identify with any of these clues?

Personal response.

(Indicate that more specific characteristics that distinguish anorexia from bulimia will be addressed in the Application portion of Session 1.)

Emotional and Perceptual Characteristics of the Eating Disordered Personality

1. Distorted body image and denial
2. Reckless Thinking (Irrational Beliefs)
   - All-or-nothing thinking
   - Overgeneralization
   - Mental filters
   - Discounting the positives
   - Jumping to conclusions
   - Mind reading
   - Magnification or minimization
   - Emotional reasoning
   - Should statements
   - Labeling
   - Blaming
3. Perfectionism
4. Low Self-Esteem
5. Depression
   - Masked anger
   - Unresolved grief/loss
6. Control
7. Dependency
8. Sexual Identity
9. Family System's Influence
   - Enmeshment
   - Rigidity
   - Overprotection
   - Conflict avoidance/detouring
   - Atmosphere
   - Inconsistency
   - High expectations
10. Sociocultural Input: Peer Pressure and Media Influence

Examples of the types of irrational beliefs include:

All-or-nothing thinking: I'll get fat if I eat that cookie. If I eat breakfast now, I'll keep eating all day.

Overgeneralization: I used to weigh a "normal" amount, and I wasn't happy. So I know gaining weight isn't going to make me feel better.

Mental filter: My husband will only love me if I'm beautiful.

Discounting the positives: So what if I got an A in chemistry; I got a C in physical education.

Jumping to conclusions: If I eat a sweet, it will be converted instantly into stomach fat. Dad is grumpy; it must be because of something I said or did.

Mind reading: Mom is really upset with me for getting a B on my chemistry test.

Magnification or minimization: I've gained two pounds, so I can't wear shorts anymore. I can't do anything right.

Emotional reasoning (confusing feelings for facts): I feel fat; therefore, I am fat.

Should statements: I should never make a mistake. I should be slender because ________ is.

Labeling: I'm a failure.

Blaming: If only I were thinner, he would love me.

Describe the characteristics to which you can relate.

Personal responses.

Indicate that most individuals who are experiencing an eating disorder tend to relate to many, sometimes even all, of the characteristics.

Spiritual Awareness Lead–In

Scripture provides admonition and encouragement for the eating disordered. To better understand God's plan for our lives and the liabilities and disobedience of engaging in eating disordered behaviors, let's examine God's Word on this subject.

Spiritual-Awareness

Allow 20–25 Minutes

Read the following scriptures and reflect on what God's viewpoint is regarding the body and food:

1 Corinthians 3:16-17

To what important building in Old Testament history does God compare the Church (the body of Christ)?

God's temple.

Who resides within every Christian?

The Holy Spirit.

What penalty does God impose on those who destroy God's temple?

"God will destroy him" (v17). This passage is referring to the entire congregation of believers as the temple of God. We destroy Christ's church by our involvement in deception, lies, rejection of truth, divisiveness, etc. When we destroy our own bodies through deception and self-lies we are also bring harm to the temple of God since we are a member of the body of Christ.

Mark 7:18-19

Does God distinguish between clean and unclean foods according to this verse?

No; He declared all foods "clean" (safe).

Why do you suppose God created food?

To provide fuel for the body.

Deuteronomy 5:6-7; Exodus 20:2-3 What is God's first commandment to His children?	To have no other god except Him.
What is the definition of a god?	A being or object believed to have more than natural attributes and powers and to require man's worship.
Have you made food and your relationship to it the god of your life?	Personal responses.
Deuteronomy 5:8; Exodus 20:4-6 What is God's second commandment to His children?	To make nothing an idol to worship.
Are you guilty of breaking this commandment by allowing your body image to be an idol which you worship?	Personal responses.
What are the consequences of breaking this commandment?	God's punishment to the third and fourth generations.
What are the rewards of keeping it?	God's love to a thousand generations.
John 6:35, 57-58 How does Jesus describe Himself in John 6:35?	As "the bread of life."
What does He say are the benefits of coming to Him?	One will never go hungry or be thirsty spiritually.
What does "coming to Him" mean to you personally?	Personal responses.
What promise are we given in John 6:57?	If we feed spiritually on Jesus, we will live eternally. Jesus came that we might "have life, and have it to the full" while we live physically and for eternity (John 10:10).
How do the consequences of feeding on manna and feeding on the *bread of life* differ?	If we eat manna only, we will die physically and spiritually. If we feed on the bread of life, we will live eternally.
What is the manna in your life?	Personal responses.

Allow 20 Minutes

What is Anorexia Nervosa?

Anorexia nervosa is an eating disorder characterized by intentional starvation associated with an intense fear of fatness which does not subside with weight loss. It is most often found among women from middle to upper socioeconomic groups, and the percentages are increasing among males. Anorexics may be extremely underweight yet insist they need to lose more weight because they see themselves as fat. The person's ability to experience hunger, fatigue, anxiety, depression, and other sensations seems to be defective and continues to worsen as she becomes increasingly malnourished. Physical findings in anorexia may include:

- A skeletal appearance.
- Extreme weight loss.
- Coarse, dry, sloughing skin.
- Fine, downy hair which may be on the back or extremities.
- Absence or suppression of menstruation.
- Reduced body fat.
- Wasting of muscles.
- Brittle hair and nails.
- Below normal heart rate, blood pressure, and body temperature.

More severe complications include abnormal heart rate and rhythm, impaired mental performance, severe malnutrition, and dehydration. Untreated physical deterioration can result in sudden death.

While it is impossible to predict the type of individual who is likely to develop anorexia nervosa, the following factors contribute to this disorder:

- Societal pressure to be thin.

- Dissatisfaction with bodies and diet which may lead to a desire to lose weight.

- Families which emphasize high achievement, perfection, and physical appearance; cannot tolerate conflict; and exert a great amount of control.

- Personality characteristics such as perfectionism, overcompliance, and high motivation but low self-esteem and manipulation.

Treatment goals for persons with anorexia focus on restoring nutritional status, normalizing eating and exercise habits, and altering attitudes toward food and body size. Treatment often requires hospitalization, especially when the weight loss is severe. Family members also need to be included in the treatment process. Christian psychotherapy concentrating on feelings about body image, weight gain, and self-esteem also must be included in the treatment.

What is Bulimia?

Bulimia is an eating disorder in which a person experiences uncontrollable, overwhelming urges to eat large quantities of food followed by self-induced vomiting, abuse of laxatives and diuretics, and/or extreme exercise. Persons with bulimia generally are aware that their eating patterns are abnormal and often conduct their behaviors secretively.

Bulimia most often is found among young women in their late teens to mid 30s. They are usually of normal weight to moderately overweight. Persons who have below normal weight caused by bulimic activity and self-induced starvation have a condition called bulimerexia.

Physical findings in bulimia may include:

- Frequent weight fluctuations.
- Irregular menstrual periods.
- Abdominal pain.
- Muscle weakness.
- Constipation.
- Diarrhea.
- Significant enlargement of the parotid glands located just below and in front of the ears.
- Damage to dental enamel.

More severe complications include electrolyte abnormalities which can lead to kidney and heart failure, inflammation of the esophagus, enlargement and rupture of the stomach, and colitis. Chronic use of syrup of ipecac to induce vomiting can be fatal.

The exact cause of bulimia is unknown, but the following factors seem to contribute to this disorder:

- Societal pressure to be thin. Excessive dieting leads to weight loss and a food-deprived state which can lead to bulimic behavior.

- Family environments where conflict, anxiety, and little structure exist. Marital dissatisfaction, general health problems, and alcoholism also are seen frequently.

- Personality characteristics include: chronic depression, problems with impulse control, low self-esteem, intolerance to frustration, and difficulty expressing feelings.

Treatment goals for persons with bulimia focus on interrupting the binge/purge cycle, normalizing eating patterns, and altering attitudes toward food, eating, and body size. Treatment may require hospitalization. Family members also should be involved in the treatment process. Christian psychotherapy is necessary to help patients understand their emotional problems and conflicts which may have originally contributed to the bulimic behavior.

Study carefully the official *DSM IV Diagnostic Criteria* for anorexia nervosa, bulimia nervosa, and eating disorders not otherwise specified and *Medical Complications of Eating Disorders* at the end of this session. If you meet the diagnostic criteria for either of these eating disorders, you are strongly encouraged to seek professional support from your physician and a Christian psychologist or psychiatrist. You are reminded that:

Seeing Yourself in God's Image is a support group, not a therapy group.

Eating disorders can be life threatening.

Guidelines for *Choosing a Therapist* and *Questions to Ask Individual Therapists, Family Therapists, and Group Therapists* are provided at the end of this session.

In John 5:1-8, Jesus asked the paralytic, "Do you want to get well?" He did not force healing on him.

How do you answer the same question?

Personal response.

Jesus healed him, and Jesus is able to heal you.

Write a prayer based on Psalm 40:1-5.

Give group members an opportunity to share their prayer if time permits.

Are you ready to say good-bye to ED (your eating disorder) and allow Jesus to preach good news to you, proclaim your freedom from the bondage of an eating disorder, give you sight, and release you from oppression?

Personal response.

Group options for contact during the week:

Introduce concept of phone list.

- Make leaders' phone numbers available the first week.
- Circulate an optional group list in the second meeting.

or

Exchange phone lists right away during Session 1.

Closing Prayer

Share prayer requests. Closing prayer might briefly lift up the requests shared by the members. As members become more comfortable in the group, encourage one of them to volunteer for closing prayer.

DSM IV Criteria for Eating Disorders

307.1 Anorexia Nervosa

A. Refusal to maintain body weight at or above a minimally normal weight for age and height (e.g., weight loss leading to maintenance of body weight less than 85 percent of that expected or failure to make expected weight gain during period of growth, leading to body weight less than 85 percent of that expected).

B. Intense fear of gaining weight or becoming fat even though underweight.

C. Disturbance in the way in which one's body weight or shape is experienced, undue influence of body weight or shape on self-evaluation, or denial of the seriousness of the current low body weight.

D. In postmenarcheal females, amenorrhea; i.e., the absence of at least three consecutive menstrual cycles. (A woman is considered to have amenorrhea if her periods occur only following hormone; e.g., estrogen administration).

Specify Type:

Restricting Type: During the current episode of anorexia nervosa, the person has not regularly engaged in binge eating or purging behavior (i.e., self-induced vomiting or the misuse of laxatives, diuretics, or enemas).

Binge Eating/Purging Type: During the current episode of anorexia nervosa, the person has regularly engaged in binge eating or purging behavior (i.e., self-induced vomiting or the misuse of laxatives, diuretics, or enemas).

307.51 Bulimia Nervosa

A. Recurrent episodes of binge eating. An episode of binge eating is characterized by both of the following:

1. Eating, in a discrete period of time (e.g., within any two-hour period), an amount of food that is definitely larger than most people would eat during a similar period of time and under similar circumstances.

2. A sense of lack of control over eating during the episode (e.g., a feeling that one cannot stop eating or control what or how much one is eating).

B. Recurrent inappropriate compensatory behavior in order to prevent weight gain, such as self-induced vomiting; misuse of laxatives, diuretics, enemas, or other medications; fasting; or excessive exercise.

C. The binge eating and inappropriate compensatory behaviors both occur, on average, at least twice a week for three months.

D. Self-evaluation is unduly influenced by body shape and weight.

E. The disturbance does not occur exclusively during episodes of anorexia nervosa.

Specify type:

Purging Type: During the current episode of bulimia nervosa, the person has regularly engaged in self-induced vomiting or the misuse of laxatives, diuretics, or enemas.

Nonpurging Type: During the current episode of bulimia nervosa, the person has used other inappropriate compensatory behaviors, such as fasting or excessive exercise, but has not regularly engaged in self-induced vomiting or the misuse of laxatives, diuretics, or enemas.

307.50 Eating Disorder Not Otherwise Specified

The Eating Disorder Not Otherwise Specified category is for disorders of eating that do not meet the criteria for any specific eating disorder. Examples include:

1. For females, all of the criteria for anorexia nervosa are met except that the individual has regular menses.

2. All of the criteria for anorexia nervosa are met except that, despite significant weight loss, the individual's current weight is in the normal range.

3. All of the criteria for bulimia nervosa are met except that the binge eating and inappropriate compensatory mechanisms occur at a frequency of less than twice a week or for a duration of less than three months.

4. The regular use of inappropriate compensatory behavior by an individual of normal body weight after eating small amounts of food (e.g., self-induced vomiting after the consumption of two cookies).

5. Repeatedly chewing and spitting out, but not swallowing, large amounts of food.

6. Binge eating disorder: Recurrent episodes of binge eating in the absence of the regular use of inappropriate compensatory behaviors characteristic of bulimia nervosa.

Research Criteria for Binge Eating Disorder

A. Recurrent episodes of binge eating. An episode of binge eating is characterized by both of the following:

   1. Eating, in a discrete period of time (for example, within any two-hour period), an amount of food that is definitely larger than most people would eat in a similar period of time under similar circumstances.

   2. A sense of lack of control over eating during the episode (for example, a feeling that one cannot stop eating or control what or how much one is eating).

B. The binge eating episodes are associated with three (or more) of the following:

   1. Eating much more rapidly than normal.

   2. Eating until feeling uncomfortably full.

   3. Eating large amounts of food when not feeling physically hungry.

   4. Eating alone because of being embarrassed by how much one is eating.

   5. Feeling disgusted with oneself, depressed, or very guilty after overeating.

C. Marked distress regarding binge eating is present.

D. The binge eating occurs, on average, at least two days a week for six months. Note: The method of determining frequency differs from that used for bulimia nervosa. Future research should address whether the preferred method of setting a frequency threshold is counting the number of days on which binges occur or counting the number of episodes of binge eating.

E. The binge eating is not associated with the regular use of inappropriate compensatory behaviors (for example, purging, fasting, excessive exercise) and does not occur exclusively during the course of anorexia nervosa or bulimia nervosa.

Medical Complications of Eating Disorders

General. The weight loss of anorexia nervosa and the binge eating, self-induced vomiting, laxative abuse, diuretic abuse, and other behaviors which can be seen both in anorexia nervosa and bulimia nervosa can have serious medical consequences.

Some specific behaviors and their consequences are:

Starvation. When people lose weight and become quite thin as is typical among patients with anorexia nervosa, most organ systems in the body stop functioning properly. If enough weight is lost, essentially all major systems in the body can malfunction. This can be quite dangerous and can be fatal. Some of the side effects are generalized, such as weakness and dizziness, while others are very specific to parts of the body. For example, at very low weights, the liver or kidneys can start to malfunction as can the heart.

Self-Induced Vomiting. Vomiting deprives the body of fluids (mainly water) and certain electrolytes (chemicals in the body). This pattern is common in people who vomit on a regular basis and can be quite dangerous. By producing a low serum potassium level, the self-induced vomiting can cause the heart to develop a sudden arrhythmia, and the patient can die. Vomiting also has other risks. Sometimes patients can tear the esophagus (the tube that joins the stomach to the mouth) while vomiting. Vomiting also damages the teeth.

Laxative Abuse. The use of laxatives to lose weight is another potentially damaging behavior. It is important to know that laxative abuse is really ineffective as a weight control technique. Some individuals believe they are losing weight or preventing food from being absorbed by using laxatives, but in reality, what they are doing is causing themselves to become dehydrated because of the loss of water in diarrhea. This dehydration can be quite dangerous. Also, laxative abuse is associated with bleeding from the gastrointestinal tract; depletion of important minerals like potassium, magnesium, and calcium; and severe problems with constipation. Rarely, individuals who abuse laxatives for long periods of time actually cause their bowels not to work properly permanently. Fortunately this complication is rare.

Diuretic Abuse. As with misuse of laxatives, the misuse of diuretics leads to fluid and electrolyte abnormalities and can thereby have more severe consequences as well, including irregularities of heart rhythm and kidney problems.

Ipecac. Ipecac is a drug which some individuals with eating disorders take to make themselves vomit. When it is used repeatedly, it can build up in the body and cause severe muscle problems and damage to the heart. Misuse of ipecac by eating-disorder patients has accounted for several fatalities. This drug is something that should never be used for weight control.

Patients often do not know when they are having problems. Some symptoms which can occur because of these complications include dizziness, experiencing the heart pounding in their chest, increased thirst, muscle cramps, noticing blood in the vomit, and feeling "foggy in the head."

Blood and Blood-Forming Elements. Anorexia nervosa is associated with a lowering of the white blood count and, in about 15 percent of cases, lowering of platelets, a blood factor necessary for proper blood clotting. This can cause bleeding problems.

Kidneys. The chronic dehydration associated with vomiting, laxative abuse, or diuretic use and with restrictive dieting can cause changes in the kidneys' ability to concentrate urine and, in rare situations, can lead to failure of the kidneys.

Metabolic Changes of Anorexia. The metabolic changes include, among others, an elevation of serum cholesterol, lowering of zinc (an important mineral), and abnormalities in liver function tests.

Stomach and GI Tract. When patients are of low weight with anorexia nervosa and/or are binge eating and vomiting frequently with bulimia nervosa, the stomach does not empty properly and secretion of fluid into the stomach is abnormally low. Therefore, many people with eating disorders feel quite bloated and uncomfortable after eating. This corrects after they eat regularly balanced meals for several weeks. Patients with eating disorders will occasionally develop swelling in the salivary glands located in the cheek muscle and in the neck.

This often appears as swelling in the cheek as if the individual has a "fat face." This is reversible with improved eating.

Heart. The fluid and electrolyte abnormalities described above or the low weight in anorexia nervosa by itself can cause abnormalities in the action of the heart muscle and in the electrical system of the heart. These can be dangerous because they can cause heart arrhythmia and death. Also, the dehydration results in low blood pressure, dizziness, and fainting.

Teeth. The vomiting in anorexia nervosa and bulimia nervosa leads to severe loss of dental enamel. When this occurs, individuals notice that their teeth will ache when exposed to hot and cold foods and liquids. This is actually one of the most common problems of patients with eating disorders.

Bone Changes. When patients are of very low weight, they absorb calcium poorly and may develop bone changes like those seen in women with osteoporosis. The long-term consequences of this are unclear, but this change may increase the risk of fractures or bone problems later in life.

Water Balance and Electrolytes. Patients engaging in eating disorder behaviors frequently develop dehydration, increased alkalinity of their blood (metabolic alkalosis), and a deficiency of serum chloride and potassium.

Hormones. When patients are of very low weight, most hormonal systems are thrown off, including the hormones that are involved in the regulation of menstrual functioning and sexual activity (resulting in amenorrhea), changes in thyroid function (with a shift away from normal thyroid activity), abnormalities of the regulation of the stress hormone cortisol (with elevated cortisol levels), and difficulties regulating blood sugar.

The good news is that most of these abnormalities appear to be readily reversible with adequate weight gain, adequate fluid intake, and cessation of binge eating, vomiting, laxative abuse, and diuretic abuse. Changes to the teeth may be permanent, and bone changes from anorexia nervosa may also pose more lasting problems.

Which of the listed complications have you noticed in yourself or been told are problems?

Choosing a Therapist

1. Ask about credentials.

2. Ask about the therapist's experience and views about treatment.
   Knowledgeable
   Compassionate
   Networked

3. Find out how much treatment will cost.

4. Inquire about billing procedures.

5. Find out the policy on missed sessions.

6. Find out about insurance reimbursement.

7. Find out the policy on family members calling the therapist.

8. Discuss what happens in a crisis.

Questions for an Individual Therapist

1. Find out how the eating behavior itself is approached in treatment. Is the eating behavior a focus of therapy, or does the therapist believe that if other issues are talked about, the eating behavior will change?

2. Is medication used? If so, when and why?

3. Will other therapies (such as group or family) be used in conjunction with the individual treatment?

4. Will a physician need to be seen? If so, how will the therapist and doctor work together? Will limits be set regarding weight and food intake? If so, how?

Questions for Family Therapists

1. How does the therapist view the eating disorder?

2. Does the therapist want to see the entire family? If so, who is included? Is it only those people living in the house, or if there is a step family, does the therapist want to see both the custodial and noncustodial families? Will this include stepparents? Will they want to see the extended family such as grandparents or important aunts and uncles? And what about young children?

3. How often will the family be seen? Once a week, every other week, or once a month?

4. In the case of family treatment of a teenage or child anorexic, what is the therapist's approach regarding parental involvement in feeding interventions?

Questions for Group Therapists

1. How is the eating disorder approached in the group? Is the group a behavior- or insight-oriented group?

2. Does the group function as a support group in which members are encouraged to call one another outside the group?

3. What are the ages of the group members? What about gender? Is the group all women, all men, or mixed?

4. Does everyone in the group have an eating disorder? If so, is the group mixed with bulimics, binge eaters, and anorexics; or are the members suffering from the same disorder?

   What to expect from treatment/therapy?

   How long will it take?

   What mood changes can be expected?

   What behavioral changes can be expected?

Session 2 Truth: A Process and a Person

Introduction

Allow 10 Minutes

Opening Prayer

Convene the group by beginning with prayer. You may choose to lead the prayer or request one or two persons to have a brief prayer. Ask God to help each member desire to know **truth**, both as a process and as the person of Jesus Christ.

Sharing Question

Truth is both a process and a person. John 8:32 reads, "You will know the truth, and the truth will set you free." In John 14:6, Jesus answered, "I am the way and the truth and the life."

When did Jesus become **truth** in your life?

or

This sharing question gives opportunity for the members to share their personal testimonies. (Unless you can extend the time for this section, responses will need to be limited to "when" rather than "how" members accepted Christ. It also, however, gives the leaders feedback on the need to incorporate a gospel presentation into the group's content.

What **truth** about God would you like to be experiencing in your life?

Personal responses. These will add further insight into the issues with which the group members are struggling.

Self-Awareness

Allow 20–25 Minutes

"I must be perfect." "I must have everyone's love and approval." "I'll be a social outcast unless I lose weight." "No one loves a fat person." "You can't eat just one______." This is just a sampling of irrational beliefs (**lies**) that can lead to unhappiness, depression, eating disordered behaviors, and all nature of nonabundant living unless taken captive, examined, and restructured. In *The Lies We Believe Workbook,* Dr. Chris Thurman, a Christian psychologist, describes a process tool for identifying and restructuring our irrational beliefs (the **lies** we believe) or, as the author of this guide likes to say, "Our Nutty Nonsense."

Our brains function like tape recorders by recording and storing the beliefs, attitudes, and expectations we have observed, heard, and appropriated as truth throughout our lives. Some of our tapes store truth ("You can't please everyone all of the time"); some store lies ("I'm only as good as what I do"). The messages stored on our tapes guide the way we feel and behave. Positive, truthful data leads to healthy behavior and feelings; negative, reckless data (thinking) leads to unhealthy behavior and feelings. Trigger events, major or minor, large or small—the events or situations that happen to us—access our tapes and, depending on the healthiness of our processing and the truth of our tapes, will either download truth or lies.

We cannot always control events and circumstances; but with tools, help, and hard work, we can control our thoughts. We can also restructure our faulty beliefs, attitudes, and expectations (erase the tapes storing lies) so there is less reckless thinking available to us. Our challenge is to make our tapes as truthful as possible thus empowering us to handle circumstances in ways that foster emotional, spiritual, and physical health.

What are your lies?

Personal response.

Chris Thurman has identified 30 prominent lies we may believe(see page 22). Along with the typical lies shared by anorexics and bulimics, they provide an opportunity for us to begin to identify the lies *we* believe.

Ask the group members to complete the self-analysis questionnaires on pages 22-23.

Spend the balance of time allocated for self-awareness sharing which lies the group selected the most.

The Lies We Believe

Do not spend too much time on any one statement, but give the answer that best describes how you really feel. Try to avoid using the neutral (4) response.

1	2	3	4	5	6	7
	strongly disagree		neutral		strongly agree	

Self Lies

___ 1. I must be perfect.
___ 2. I must have everyone's love and approval.
___ 3. It is easier to avoid problems than to face them.
___ 4. Things have to go my way for me to be happy.
___ 5. My unhappiness is externally caused.

Worldly Lies.

___ 6. I can have it all.
___ 7. I am only as good as what I do.
___ 8. Life should be easy.
___ 9. Life should be fair.
___ 10. I shouldn't have to wait for what I want.
___ 11. People are basically good.

Marriage Lies

___ 12. My marriage problems are my spouse's fault.
___ 13. If my marriage takes hard work, my spouse and I must not be right for each other.
___ 14. My spouse should meet all my needs.
___ 15. My spouse owes me for what I have done for him/her.
___ 16. I shouldn't have to change who I am in order to make my marriage better.
___ 17. My spouse should be like me.

Distortion Lies

___ 18. I often make mountains out of molehills.
___ 19. I often take things personally.
___ 20. Things are black and white to me.
___ 21. I often miss the forest for the trees.
___ 22. The past predicts the future.
___ 23. I often reason things out with my feelings rather than with the facts.

Religious Lies

___ 24. God's love can be earned.
___ 25. God hates the sin and the sinner.
___ 26. Because I'm a Christian, God will protect me from pain and suffering.
___ 27. All of my problems are caused by my sins.
___ 28. It is my Christian duty to meet all the needs of others.
___ 29. Painful emotions such as anger, depression, and anxiety are signs that my faith in God is weak.
___ 30. God can't use me unless I am spiritually strong.

(Thurman, *Workbook*, pp. 3-4, section headings added.)

Eating-Disordered Reckless Thinking

Check all that apply.

___ 1. The worst thing that could happen to me would be to gain weight or become fat.

___ 2. My favorite escape from my problems is food. If I give up this area of my life, I'll have to deal with all those sore spots, and I don't want to.

___ 3. I'm happy with my life the way it is.

___ 4. I need to be good at everything.

___ 5. I should never make a mistake.

___ 6. I must earn my happiness. I don't deserve it.

___ 7. Other people are more important than I am.

___ 8. If you are not slender, you should be angry at yourself.

___ 9. You'll be a social outcast unless you lose weight.

___10. Appearance is a woman's most important personal attribute.

___11. I have to continue this pattern because my friends won't care about me if I'm well and don't have this problem anymore.

___12. The best way to stay thin is the way I'm doing it now.

___13. My eating disorder doesn't affect other people.

___14. I don't want to try to quit this behavior because I know it will just happen again.

___15. If I give up my eating disorder, I'll have nothing to blame rejection on.

___16. I don't want sensual advances. If I give up my eating disorder, I may become more appealing. This way I can avoid my sexuality.

___17. My family is constantly on me about what I eat, but at least they pay attention to me.

Spiritual Awareness Lead-In

2 Corinthians 10:5b admonishes us to "take captive every thought to make it obedient to Christ." In this session we will be learning a process and acquiring a tool which will help us do just that. Before we look at **truth** as a process, let's focus on **the truth**—Jesus Christ. How often do we trust in our own thoughts, feelings, experiences, and expertise or the input of others outside ourselves to be the source of truth for our lives? Jesus said *He* is the truth. We can never know the truth of our worth, our circumstances, our wants and needs, our rights and responsibilities, or our purpose/mission unless we first hear truth from Jesus, the author of truth. It is one thing to know *about* truth. It is quite different to experience truth as we allow God to work in and through our lives. God's truth will have no impact on you until and unless you have first accepted Jesus Christ **as** truth and then look to Him **for** truth. No doubt we have observed, heard of, or read of those whose lives have been impacted, made whole, through the working of God in their lives. But have you asked, "Have I allowed God to be **truth** in my life?"

Spiritual-Awareness

Allow 20–25 Minutes

Read the following scriptures and reflect on what God says about truth.

John 8:32
What does this verse tell us is the result of knowing truth?

This scripture indicates that freedom from bondage results from knowing and acting on truth.

John 8:36
What does this verse tell us about how freedom from bondage is obtained?

This verse tells us who sets us free from the bondage of wrong thinking. It is Jesus Christ.

Romans 12:2
Why are we commanded to renew our minds?

Transformation of our minds is the key to not conforming to the world's view of truth.

2 Corinthians 10:3-6
How does the Christian achieve right and truthful thinking?

Living the abundant Christian life is like being engaged in warfare. We live in the world but fight with spiritual weapons which give us the power to break down strongholds (beliefs and positions which are so embedded we sense we are helpless and hopeless to break them). Right thinking comes from taking every thought captive to make it obedient to Christ (i.e., we ask ourselves what/how would Christ think in this situation).

Philippians 4:8-9
What does Paul admonish us about our thoughts?

The Apostle Paul admonishes us to focus on true and right thinking and identifies further categories of right thinking for us (noble, pure, lovely, admirable, excellent, praiseworthy).

John 14:6
How does Jesus fit into the **truth** system?

This verse reminds us that truth is not only what we think but **who we know**.

Application

Allow 20 Minutes

How then do we "take every thought captive"? How do we develop the mind of Christ so we can think rightly and truthfully? This section of our session focuses on learning and using a tool developed by Chris Thurman called *The Truth System.*

T — Triggering Event
R — Reckless Thinking
U — Unhealthy Behavior/Feelings
T — Truthful Thinking
H — Healthy Behavior/Feelings

Each letter of the acronym, **TRUTH**, stands for an important part of the process of achieving emotional, spiritual, and physical health and maturity.

Summarize the TRUTH system in the entire Application section and then ask the group members to identify major and minor trigger devices they have experienced. Next, follow the instructions at the bottom of page 27.

The first T, *triggering event,* is the part of the **TRUTH** system where reality shows up. Reality may be a minor or major event. Examples of major trigger events include death of a loved one, divorce, injury or illness, marriage, job loss. Small weight gain, interruptions, too many things to do, delays, and lost or misplaced items are examples of minor trigger events.

Ask group members to identify at least one major and one minor trigger they have experienced in their lives.

Skipping R for the moment, U is the part of the **TRUTH** system where our reaction to the trigger events occurs. Our reactions are usually physiological, emotional, and/or behavioral. Physiological reactions to trigger events include but are not limited to fatigue, dizziness, insomnia, headaches, stomach problems, etc. Emotional reactions include but again are not limited to anxiety, depression, anger, guilt, resentment, sadness, etc. Among the possible behavioral reactions are withdrawing, yelling, overworking, restricting food intake, binge-eating, etc.

Ask the group to identify some of their unhealthy physiological, emotional, and behavioral reactions to the trigger events they identified earlier.

The T causes U Problem: One of the most destructive mistakes we can make is believing that trigger events (T) directly cause our unhealthy reactions (U). For example, if your father makes a comment to you while standing in line to attend a movie that the young woman at the popcorn counter is too heavy, you might skip dinner that evening. You might conclude that your father's comments caused you to skip dinner. Trigger events do not directly cause our reactions however. People often experience exactly the same event but react to it in much different ways. We also know biblically that T causes U is a lie "For as he thinks in his heart, so is he" (Proverbs 23:7 NAS). That verse does not say, "As what happens, so he is." Events do not directly cause reactions. It is how we *think* about the event that will determine our physiological, emotional, and behavioral responses.

Backing up to R, this is the part of the TRUTH system where we think about the trigger event that has just occurred (or which historically has not been dealt with). As stated earlier but can never be overstated, the way you think about an event will determine your physiological, emotional, and behavioral reaction(s) to it. When you think lies, your reactions to trigger events will be inappropriate and unhealthy. When you think truth, your reactions to trigger events will be appropriate and healthy.

Before taking a look at T, R, U in action, let us review several forms of the most harmful, distorted/reckless thinking:

1. All or Nothing: Looking at situations, beliefs, expectations in absolute, black and white categories.
2. Overgeneralization: Viewing a negative event as a never-ending pattern of defeat.
3. Mental Filter: Dwelling on the negatives and ignoring the positives.
4. Discounting the Positives: Insisting that your accomplishments or positive qualities do not count.
5. Jumping to Conclusions: Concluding things are bad without any definite evidence.
6. Mind Reading: The most prominent form of jumping to conclusions by assuming you know what others are thinking or feeling.
7. Magnification or Minimization: Blowing things way out of proportion or shrinking their importance.
8. Emotional Reasoning: Concluding from feelings without considering facts.
9. "Should" Statements: Criticizing self or others with "shoulds," "shouldn'ts," "musts," "oughts," and "have-tos."

10. Labeling: Assigning a name to oneself rather than identifying the behavior (e.g., "I'm a loser" rather than "I made a mistake").
11. Blaming: Blaming oneself for something you were not responsible for or blaming others and overlooking ways you contributed to a problem.

Here is an example of T, R, U at work:

T Eating out with friends. One comments, "I thought you were on a diet."

R "She and everyone else must think I need to be on a diet."

U Continues to restrict eating. Constant preoccupation with the friend's comment. Feels anxious, depressed, and fatigued.

The second T stands for truthful thinking. If you find you get into *reckless thinking*, take it captive and reframe, restructure, face the real truth.

The second T in the example above might go something like this:

T I am doing something out of the norm for me. I'm eating with my friends in a restaurant. No one but me probably even noticed the comment. Marcie was just responding to what she's observed about me. I often don't eat when we're out together.

We are now able to finish out the acronym with H for healthy behavior/feelings. After you tell yourself the truth, you can respond to a trigger event in a healthy way:

H Enjoys her evening with her friends, eats the meal she orders, recognizes that her friends do not think she is fat, and acknowledges to herself that she is not fat. Feels energetic for the basketball game they attend together.

With consistent practice and application of the TRUTH system, most unhealthy thoughts, practices, and feelings, not just those related to eating disorders, can be taken captive to obedience to Christ which leads to abundant living.

Use the balance of the Application time for group members to practice the TRUTH system. Ask for a volunteer to work through the system as you, the leader, write the steps on a white board. Encourage the group members to help one another identify what the reckless thinking might be and how to reframe it into truthful thinking.

Ask group members to practice the TRUTH system during the week and to bring an example to share at the beginning of the next session.

In Preparation for Session 3:
Bring a camera to this session to photograph the group members.

Ask the group to identify one member they all can agree to *see* as normal size. (This most often is one of the co-leaders who either has not experienced an eating disorder or who is in recovery.)

Photograph each member individually standing beside the *normal* group member. At the next session, distribute the pictures to each member and ask them to make observations about their picture.

Closing Prayer

Share prayer requests (members' opportunity to support one another throughout the week).

Pray for the prayer requests as well as anything else you heard mentioned during the meeting. Invite the group members to join you in the prayers if they wish.

Session 3 *Distorted Body Image and Denial*

Introduction

Allow 10 Minutes

Opening Prayer

Ask God to help each member to be clear in her thinking. Ask Him to help each member persevere in His love.

Sharing Question

How have you become more aware of reckless thinking in your life this week? Describe.

Personal response.

or

How have you taken reckless thinking captive?

Personal response. Ask group members to share examples of how they have practiced using the TRUTH system.

The feminine pronoun is used in the text; however, males are also subject to eating disorders and the percentages are gradually increasing.

Self-Awareness

Allow 20-25 Minutes

Eating disordered thinking and behaving trigger and are triggered by distorted body images and denial of actual body size and shape.

Share pictures taken during Session 2.

Let us make observations about our size and shape using the *normal* group member with whom the picture was made as a point of reference.

This activity helps objectify the group members' interpretation of their size and shape and thus reduces distortion. It may be necessary to provide a ruler so the member can actually measure the size of various body parts in relationship to the "normal" group member.

Assessment of preoccupation with food and one's body image and how this preoccupation creates/maintains distortion: Preoccupation with food and one's body image is counter to God's will for our lives. This preoccupation makes food our god and our body image an idol which is counter to two of God's commandments (Deuteronomy 5:6-8). (See Session 1: *Spiritual Awareness.*)

Assess your preoccupation by going through the following questions:

1. Do you feel extremely guilty after eating?
2. If you gain a pound, do you worry that you will keep on gaining?
3. Do you think about dieting a lot?
4. Are you terrified of gaining weight?
5. Do you exaggerate the importance of slimness?
6. Do you prepare meals for others which you yourself do not eat?
7. Do you keep secret hoards of food?
8. Are you concerned about how others see and react to your body size?
9. Do you feel nervous eating sweets and carbohydrates? Other foods?
10. Do you have fears about never being able to stop eating?
11. Do you look at yourself in the mirror numerous times daily?
12. Do you look forward to binges?
13. Do your concerns about food, diet, body, and weight ever distract you from business at hand?
14. Have you ever waited for discarded food or eaten garbage?
15. Have you concealed vomit?
16. Do you weigh yourself often (e.g., daily)?
17. Do your career choices reflect your eating disorder?
18. Do you think about your stomach, thighs, buttocks, hips, or waist as being too large or the wrong shape?
19. Do you have special meals/food combinations/binges that have special significance to you?

20a. Are you dissatisfied with your body?
20b. Does this affect your day-to-day state of well-being?

For the purpose of group sharing, ask members to simply circle the number of questions they answer *yes* to and total them. After the group has completed their tally, allow time to share *how* preoccupied they are (i.e. number of yes responses) and discuss any particularly prevalent preoccupations.

Spiritual Awareness Lead-In

An idol can be described as a *God substitute.* According to Isaiah 44:20, idols bring about a deluded heart.

How might an eating disorder be a delusion?

A lie (eating disorder) can be in one's right hand, and she cannot see it.

Read the following scriptures and note the importance of our bodies in God's view.

1 Corinthians 6:19-20
To whom do our bodies belong and why?

Another passage identifying the body as the temple of the Holy Spirit, this one also focuses on the price Christ paid to redeem us. It indicates to whom we belong, including our bodies.

Genesis 1:27
According to this verse, whose image is reflected each time we look in the mirror?

This verse establishes our image as being created in the image of God, an awesome truth to acknowledge (as well as an awesome image to see each time we look in the mirror).

Psalm 139:13-14a
What does the Psalmist acknowledge in these verses regarding the formation of and nature of our bodies?

These verses remind us that God formed our inmost being in our mother's womb with the blueprint and time line for our entire life already planned by Him and known by Him.

Romans 12:1-2
What do these verses urge us to do and why?

These verses urge us to offer our bodies as living sacrifices to God. We do this as an act of worship, and we are able to symbolically present our bodies as holy and pleasing if and because we renew our minds with truth (i.e., are not conformed to the thinking of the world).

Colossians 2:20-23
What does this passage tell us about *food rules*?

This passage is a reminder of the falsehood of worldly food rules.

Application

Allow 20 Minutes

Thus far, we have focused on how you think and feel about your body size and parts.This Application centers on becoming more accepting of the body you have right now.

Acceptance of your body is a daily process of perspective. One day you may feel fat and unattractive, and the next day you may feel slim and pretty even though your body has essentially not changed. Identifying and challenging your negative thoughts and feelings about your body and keeping God's view of your body in mind are instrumental and essential to accepting yourself and your body.

What are frequent negative thoughts you have about your body size and shape?

Personal responses.

Challenge each of these thoughts. (Identify the *Reckless Thinking* from the **TRUTH** system presented in Session 2.)

In addition to challenging the negative thoughts about your body, focus on what functions your body is capable of.

Personal responses.

What does your body allow you to do?

Personal responses.

1. Example: walk and talk
2.
3.

What does your body allow you to enjoy?

1. Example: see colors, hear music
2.

Set one goal for the week regarding eating behaviors or thought patterns.

Remind group members that the goals and prayer requests are to be kept confidential.

Share the goal with the group for accountability purposes and for prayer support.

Refer often this week to the *Survival Notes for Body Image* at the end of this session.

Closing Prayer

Pray for the needs you heard expressed during the meeting. Be sure to invite others to pray as well.

Survival Notes for Body Image

DOs

1. Do accept that bodies come in a variety of shapes and sizes.

2. Do remember that we can be our own worst critics and that others really find us attractive.

3. Do allow for normal variations in weight and shape.

4. Do explore your *internal* self—emotionally, spiritually, and as a growing human being.

5. Do recognize your strengths in terms of your appearance (parts of your body that you like) and your personal qualities (caring, enthusiastic, honest, etc.).

6. Do decide how you wish to spend your energy—pursuing the "perfect" image or focusing on your spiritual growth and your personal and interpersonal needs.

7. Do remember that attractiveness comes from within; feeling positive about yourself will affect how others view you.

8. Do be aware of your own weight prejudice and explore how it interferes with your self-esteem.

9. Do find ways to pamper yourself and treat your body with the respect it deserves.

DON'Ts

1. Don't let your body (your tent: 2 Corinthians 5:1) define who you are.

2. Don't let obsession with your body keep you from closeness with God and others.

3. Don't forget that society changes its view of what is "beautiful" over time, but God's view of beauty never changes.

4. Don't believe that thinness is the same as happiness.

5. Don't be afraid to ask others for support.

6. Don't be afraid to actually enjoy your body; i.e., the functions of your body parts (your legs allow you to walk), not just how they look.

Session 4 The Family System's Influence

Introduction

Allow 10 Minutes

Opening Prayer

Pray for the group that the Holy Spirit will provide knowledge during the meeting and that the knowledge of the truths of God might penetrate beyond the mind and into the heart.

Sharing Questions

We ended Session 3 by setting and sharing a goal for the week regarding eating behaviors or thought patterns.

What was your goal for last week?

Personal response.

Did you meet your goal? How or how not?

Personal response.

What support/accountability do you need from the group regarding this goal?

Personal response.

Self-Awareness

Allow 20-25 Minutes

Are families of the eating disordered different from other families?

Yes.

Are there characteristics that describe and distinguish the eating disordered family?

Yes.

Both the individual and her family is *eating disordered.* An eating disorder is a family system's problem. The following five diagnostic characteristics are evident in practically every *eating disordered family:*

- Enmeshment
- Rigidity
- Overprotection
- Conflict avoidance/detouring
- An atmosphere of inconsistency and/or high expectations

Each of these characteristics relates to unhealthy *boundaries.* Enmeshment characterizes the lack of boundaries. Members of an eating disordered family are unable to identify where one family member ends and another begins. In contrast, when boundaries are attempted within this enmeshment, they are so rigid no one dares question the rules or consider *coloring outside the lines* less the enmeshment be challenged.

Overprotection is used to maintain the enmeshment and limit growth and development toward emancipation from the family and the taking on of separate adult roles. Because there is little or no *give and take* in the eating disordered family, conflict is totally avoided or detoured, or so it would *appear.* The absence of conflict resolution skills or the willingness to develop any of these skills leaves only the option of not acknowledging there is conflict, again fueling the enmeshment.

Finally, all of the above is maintained via an atmosphere of inconsistency and/or high expectations. What appears to be a family *in control* is a family totally *out of control* (out of boundaries). To symbolically survive all this masked chaos, the eating disordered individual attempts to establish control somewhere, somehow, and finds that the eating disordered behavior gives a pretense of doing just that. Ironically, the eating disordered behavior only reinforces the dysfunctional behavior of the family.

The authors of *The Thin Disguise* describe five types of dysfunctional families which foster the following negative influences:

- An abnormal desire to please people.
- An inability to cope with painful feelings.
- A lack of the ability to *be oneself.*
- An unhealthy defense mechanism—splitting.*
- Low impulse control or *I want it now!*

* The individual learns to split herself into the good part and the bad part with constant fear that the bad part will gain control. Becoming stuck at the compartmentalization stage, she views everything as good or bad (black or white thinking).

Read the characteristics of the five types of dysfunctional families: the upside down family, the perfectionistic family, the controlling family, the rageaholic family, and the rigid family (see *Types of Dysfunctional Families* on pages 40-41).

Identify the five eating disordered family characteristics in each of these family types. See page 34.

Examples.

Which of the five eating disordered family characteristics can you identify in your family? Share examples with the group.

Examples.

Which of the dysfunctional family types best describes your family? Why?

Examples.

Vredevelt, Pam, et al., *The Thin Disguise.* (Nashville, TN: Thomas Nelson), 1992. Used with permission.

Spiritual Awareness Lead-In

We grow up in an earthly family, but as Christians, we are also members of the family of God. God is our Father; Christ is our brother. God's many names represent His roles in our life:

El Elyon—the sovereign ruler of the universe
El Roi—the God who sees
El Shaddai—our all-sufficient one
Adonai—Lord and Master
Jehovah—the self-existent one
Jehovah-Jireh—our provider
Jehovah-Nissi—our banner
Jehovah-Mekoddishkem—the Lord who sanctifies
Jehovah-Shalom—the God of peace
Jehovah-Sabbath—the God who meets failure and provides deliverance
Jehovah-Raah—my shepherd
Jehovah-Tsidkenu—the Lord our righteousness
Jehovah-Shammah—the Lord who is there
Jehovah-Rapha—the Lord who **heals** (physical infirmities, illnesses of the mind, and illnesses of the soul)

Spiritual-Awareness

Allow 20-25 Minutes

The focus of this Spiritual Awareness section is on the healing role of God, our Father.

Exodus 15:22-27

What promise did God make to His people in this passage?

He would not bring on them any of the diseases the Egyptians experienced.

What were His expectations of them?

God expected them to listen carefully for His voice, to do what He taught them to be right, to "pay attention," and to obey His decrees.

What might the "piece of wood" represent? (Hint: What New Testament event might it foreshadow?)

Could it be that the piece of wood which made the water sweet is a picture of the cross?

---

2 Chronicles 7:14

What does this verse tell us about God's willingness to heal and His conditions for healing?

God is willing to heal if we will humble ourselves, seek His face, pray, and cease from dysfunctional behavior.

Psalm 103:1-5

In this hymn to God's love and compassion toward His people, what personal benefits is the Psalmist celebrating?

He forgives our sins, heals all our diseases, redeems our life from the "pit," crowns us with love and compassion, and satisfies our desires with good things.

Matthew 8:16-17

The healings of the demon-possessed in this passage are an example of what greater role of Christ as prophesied by Isaiah?

He took up our infirmities and carried our diseases to the cross.

Luke 4:18

What does this verse tell us about Jesus?

Jesus preached the good news to the poor, proclaimed freedom for prisoners, recovered sight for the blind, released the oppressed, and proclaimed the year of the Lord's favor.

Which area from this passage are you most in need of in your life right now ? Why?

Personal response.

---

1 Peter 2:24-25

How did Jesus provide for our healing?

He bore our sins on the cross and died for us. By His wounds, we are healed.

Application

Allow 20 Minutes

Select as many of these Application activities to complete as the group time allows:

Provide blank pieces of paper and different color markers or crayons.

Draw a picture (sketch) of your family at dinner when you were young.

Each person takes a blank piece of paper on which to draw their family eating dinner when they were a child. (For example, if the family ate around a table, draw the table with each member sitting there. If people ate in different locations, draw where they ate. Note: This is not intended to be a "work of art," only a rough outline.)

Use different color markers or crayons to represent each person's usual mood. (For example, if mom was usually angry, draw her with a red marker; and if brother was generally depressed, draw him with a blue marker.)

To illustrate the communication patterns between people, use varied lines between them. (For example, if mom and dad yelled a lot, draw a jagged line between them. If two sisters were close, draw a straight line connecting them. If you and your dad hardly ever talked or weren't emotionally connected, don't draw a line connecting you and your dad at all.)

Hold your drawing up for the rest of the group to see.

- Explain why each person is whatever color they are and what the communication patterns between people were.
- Talk about the family mealtime rules. (For example, did you have to finish everything on your plate? Did whoever eat the fastest get the most? Who cooked?)
- Share any other observations or important information about the influence of the family on your relationship with food.

Identify your family's influence on your thoughts:

How did your family view the use of food?

Personal response.

What were the effects of those views on your current beliefs about weight and food?

Personal response.

Read Psalm 27:10-11.

How do these verses apply to your family's circumstances?

Personal response.

Encourage each group member to update her goal for the week regarding eating behaviors or thought patterns.

Also, update prayer requests, including prayers for healing of the *family system's* influences.

Closing Prayer

Pray about specific needs and struggles mentioned during sharing times. Thank God for all we have and all we are in Christ.

Types of Dysfunctional Families

The Upside Down Family

In this family, the child meets the emotional needs of the parents—primarily the mother rather than the other way around. At the same time, the father's love must often be earned by the daughter's (son's) behavior. This situation teaches the child that her own needs are not nearly as important as those of her parents since her parents are vital for the survival of the family. As the child learns to suppress and deny her needs, she eventually becomes so out of touch with those needs that by the time she reaches adolescence, she is no longer aware of what her needs are. At this point, her unmet needs are so tremendous she begins to fall apart and demand that someone give her attention. The onset of an eating disorder often takes place at this time.

Upside down families are usually middle class to upper middle class; the children's physical and financial needs are adequately met. However, both parents often severely neglect emotional needs.

The unwritten rules in an upside-down family are:

The child should meet the emotional needs of the parent or parents.
Self-sacrifice is the prized quality.
The child learns to deny her needs and feelings.

The Perfectionistic Family

In healthy families, children are taught to excel, to capitalize on their strengths, to recognize their weaknesses, and to recover and learn from their mistakes. In the dysfunctional family, each member must be an overachiever, never falling short in anything—standards that are, of course, impossible to achieve.

This family has a need to be regarded as all good and picture perfect. The greatest emphasis is on the *family appearance.* Focus is also often on body appearance.

In perfectionistic families, children are told, "Just do the best you can"; but when they do the best they can, it is not quite good enough.

The unwritten rules in a perfectionistic family are:

Every family member must *measure up.*
Every family member must make the family look great.
Every family member can have only positive feelings.
Every family member must look good on the outside at all times.
The child learns, "I'm unacceptable if I'm not perfect."

The Controlling Family

A healthy level of protection is necessary for the nurturing and survival of any family. A dysfunctional family carries it to extremes. In an anorexic's family, children are sometimes overprotected. They have different rules from those of their friends. They are smothered in an effort to control every possible danger or problem.

Parents in a controlling family are often trying to live their lives through their children. They have "unfinished business"—a major goal, need, or expectation that was not fulfilled in their own pasts which they are passing on to the next generation.

Parents in controlling families often exert influence through guilt and shame. "You are so fortunate your mother and I are willing to ______________." In some cases both parents are controlling; in others, only one parent.

Hostile control comes most often from the mother and may be in the form of overt or covert control. It can include yelling, screaming, or hysteria over something as minor as leaving a wet towel on the floor. Yet there is little consistency in that the same infraction may cause no reaction whatsoever the following day.

The unwritten rules in a controlling family are:

The parents' unfinished business becomes the child's business.
Parents assume it is okay to control the family through guilt and shame.
The child learns, "My feelings and thoughts or opinions don't count. It is wrong to have them."

The Rageaholic Family

In the rageaholic family, only the parent or one parent is allowed to express feelings. The predominant feeling is obviously rage or anger. Unfortunately, the children are taught to believe they are responsible for that anger. Mothers in rageaholic families may have anger and rage from the family of origin, and in some cases, the daughter becomes an "emotional receptacle" for that rage. Although the mother is, in actuality, angry with herself and her parents, she pushes that anger onto her daughter.

The unwritten rules in a rageaholic family are:

Parents are the only ones who are permitted to have feelings.
The child is responsible for the parents' rage.
The unspoken standard is it is okay to abuse a child when a parent is angry.
The child learns to repress her anger completely.

The Rigid Family

Healthy families are warm and affectionate. Rules, as well as people, are flexible. In dysfunctional families flexibility is a nonexistent concept, and affection is seldom expressed. The father especially tends to be obsessive about the standards in the family. There is no warmth, no emotion. Each family member should be able to take care of himself or herself. This is called emotional neglect.

The unwritten rules in a rigid family are:

As long as a child's physical needs are being met, the child is okay. The child's emotional needs are not considered.
Nurturing—hugging, kissing, or saying "I love you"—is wrong.
Family members are supposed to take care of themselves.
The child believes that emotions and longings are wrong.

Session 5 Breaking Free from Social Pressures

Introduction

Allow 10 Minutes

Opening Prayer

Pray that the group members may be strengthened by understanding their identity *in Christ*. Pray that each person will be freed of destructive social pressures.

Sharing Question

What have you learned about yourself this past week?

or

How are you *thinking* of yourself today? Is your thinking *reckless* or *truthful?*

Personal response.

Self-Awareness

Allow 20 – 25 Minutes

Eating disorders are triggered by multiple factors; cultural, individual, and family factors contribute to their development in different ways for different individuals. For several decades the fashion, entertainment, and publishing industries have bombarded women with role models for physical attractiveness which are so gaunt they represent virtually no women in the actual population. This has resulted in restrictive eating, dangerous food related behaviors, and increased vulnerability to eating disorders.

The social norms for attractiveness presented in women's magazines, movies, and on television have consistently woven the image of *fitness* and *acceptability* into the slender shape ideal. The health benefits of exercise are real, but its promotion as a weight loss strategy is distorted. Dieting and exercise appear to be a clear ticket to acceptability and personal happiness. In addition to dieting to enhance physical "attractiveness," in Western culture, athletes participating in sports that emphasize leanness for performance are also exposed to more pressure to diet and hence are at greater risk for eating disorders. (Athletics, especially wrestling, is a great risk factor for the development of eating disorders in males.)

Other cultural risk factors such as role conflicts experienced by women may also be implicated in the development of eating disorders. In general, when women experience some kind of failure, especially relationship failures, they attribute that failure to their weight. They think that if they can control their weight, they will be able to get what they want or need.

Culturally, men and women talk about their bodies differently. "Research has shown that men tend to evaluate their bodies realistically and their self-appraisals match the appraisals of others" (Pipher, p. 16). In contrast, women, as a group, consistently see themselves as fatter and less attractive than others see them. Female friends also often play a role in the development of each other's eating disorders by "teaching" them that "if you throw up, you won't gain weight."

College females, stressed by academic and social pressures and eager for male approval, tend to be hypercritical of their bodies. Many bulimics are women with traditional values who have accepted society's definition of their roles. Eating disorders often become the *rebellion of choice* for Christian young women. Their values negate sex, drugs, and alcohol, but it is morally safe, they consciously or unconsciously conclude, to *act out* with food.

> At one time, I thought that family systems' theories were the most useful ways to look at anorexia. At this point, however, I've seen more and more anorexic girls coming from stable families—and I think the cultural theories may be more important. These cultural theories seem to best explain the enormous rise in the incidence rates of anorexia (Pipher, p. 74).

Given the profound cultural pressures on women to diet, it is important to ask why all women do not develop some level of disordered eating. This fact alone is support for the multiple factors influence (cultural, family, and individual factors) in the development of eating disorders.

Using a *finger voting technique*, we will poll our participation in the list of "typically unhealthy cultural attitudes" below:

If your response is:

NEVER	Raise your fist
RARELY	Raise 1 finger
OCCASIONALLY	Raise 2 fingers
FREQUENTLY	Raise 3 fingers
ALMOST DAILY	Raise 4 fingers
DAILY	Raise 5 fingers

How often do you:

- Talk about your appearance.
- Talk about someone else's appearance.
- Admire slenderness.
- Talk about exercise for weight control/loss.
- Admire obsessive exercise.
- Talk about your weight.
- Talk about someone else's weight.
- Talk about calories.
- Talk about how little you have eaten or your diet.
- Encourage perfectionism.
- Encourage conformity instead of self-determination and freedom.
- Criticize someone.

Which of the attitudes are most prevalent for the group members?

See Application section for additional activity with this information.

Spiritual Awareness Lead–In

The Apostle Paul encourages us to be free of sociocultural influences that are contrary to God's will. He states, "Do not conform any longer to the pattern of this world, but be transformed by the renewing of your mind" (Romans 12:2). To be transformed is a process, not a single event.

What is the result of a "renewed mind"?

Right thinking.

Spiritual-Awareness

Allow 20 - 25 Minutes

In this session we are focusing on the following sociocultural influences that are risk factors for the development of an eating disorder:

Appearance
Exercise
Calories
Perfectionism
Criticism

Slenderness
Weight
Diets
Conformity

Let's now look at what the Word of God provides as spiritual encouragement for the prevention of an eating disorder.

Genesis 1 and 2 tell how God created Adam and Eve in His image and make it clear that besides the physical life we inherited from Adam (and which the sociocultural influences above attempt to destroy), we also inherited the capacity for spiritual life (review Genesis 1:27 from Session 3).

For the Christian, to be spiritually alive is to be united with God by being in Christ. Neil Anderson states in the book *Victory Over the Darkness* that union with God provides three important conditions for believers:

Significance: (a) The dominion that Adam exercised before the Fall has been restored to you as a Christian. (b) As a child of God, you have important work to do for your Lord. (c) As part of your inheritance in Christ, Satan has no authority over you.

What do each of the following verses tell us about our *significance* in Christ?

1 Corinthians 3:16	I am God's temple (the temple of the Holy Spirit).
John 15:1, 5	I am a branch of the true vine.
John 15:16	I have been chosen and appointed to bear fruit.
Ephesians 2:6	I am seated with Christ in heaven.
Ephesians 2:10	I am God's workmanship.
Ephesians 3:12	I may approach God with freedom and confidence.
Philippians 4:13	I can do all things through Christ who gives me the strength.

Safety and Security: Adam was completely cared for in the garden. Likewise, we who follow Christ lack for nothing.

What do the following verses tell us about our safety and security in Christ?

John 10:27-29	I have eternal life in Christ, and no one or nothing can take that from me.
Romans 8:1-2	I am free forever from condemnation.
Romans 8:28	I am assured that all things work together for good.
Romans 8:35	I cannot be separated from the love of God.
Philippians 1:6	I am confident that the good work God has begun in me will be completed.
2 Timothy 1:7	I have not been given a spirit of fear but of power, love, and self-discipline.
1 John 5:18	I am born of God and the evil one cannot touch me.

Belonging: A true sense of belonging comes not only from knowing that we belong to God but also from belonging to each other.

What do the following verses tell us about acceptance and belonging?

John 1:12	I am God's child.
John 15:15	I am Christ's friend.
1 Corinthians 6:17	I am united with the Lord, and I am one spirit with Him.
1 Corinthians 6:19-20	I have been bought with a price. I belong to God.
Ephesians 1:5	I have been adopted as God's child.
Colossians 1:14	I have been redeemed and forgiven of all my sins.
Colossians 2:10	I am complete in Christ.

Based on these three important spiritual influences on our lives, how do the following verses encourage us to *do* life?

Colossians 2:20-23	We are encouraged not to follow such world rules as "Do not taste" which are not based on true spiritual wisdom.
Ephesians 4:17-18, 22, 24	Paul *insists* that we not think futilely (as the Gentiles were doing) but rather to put off our *old self* and to put on the *new self* created to be like God (made righteous and holy through our position in Christ).
2 Corinthians 10:3-5 With what weapons are we to *fight*?	Divine spiritual weapons (as opposed to the weapons of the world).

Ephesians 6:13-18
What weapons are identified in these verses?

The armor of God:
- Belt of Truth
- Breastplate of Righteousness
- Feet Shod with the Gospel of Peace
- Shield of Faith
- Helmet of Salvation
- Sword of the Spirit (Word of God)
- Prayer

Application

Allow 20 Minutes

Complete one or both of the following Application activities:

Make a chart dividing your life into key periods such as infancy, elementary school, high school, first job, college, early marriage, first child, last child, empty nest, menopause, postmenopause, retirement, widowhood, or any other divisions that are appropriate in your lifeline.

Provide paper for this activity.

Reflect on how you felt about yourself during each of those time periods (e.g., content, energetic, anxious, excited, depressed).

What sociocultural influences contributed to your development of those feelings?

What have you learned in this session to encourage you to erase those influences?

After completing your lifeline, share your insights with the group members.

Personal response.

The Self-Awareness section of this session addressed the food and physical characteristics that are subject to unhealthy cultural attitudes:

Appearance	Slenderness
Exercise	Weight
Calories	Diets
Perfectionism	Conformity
Criticism	

Let's look more closely at these areas and consider strategies for change.

If time permits, ask group members to share briefly their strategies for change. If time does not permit, you may want to summarize the information for the group members to bring closure. The group members should have already done this activity in the workbook.

Appearance—Talking about appearance is natural, but it is excessive in our culture. Focus on appearance encourages the development of exaggerated concern about body weight and size. Focus instead on the importance of health, happiness, and character.

Slenderness—Appreciating the physical beauty of slender people is fine provided you do not promote the idea that slenderness is a prerequisite for beauty. Focus on internal beauty and the uniqueness of each individual. Minimize all appearance-oriented comments and/or evaluations.

Exercise—Regular exercise is a great way to promote good health and well-being, but extreme exercising for weight control is unhealthy. Make exercise a personal choice for having fun and feeling good.

Weight—Discussions about weight can be positive if they refute popular myths or appreciate how helpful and healthy it has been for someone to stop dieting and maintain a comfortable, stable weight. Avoid weight discussions that provoke shame or encourage unhealthy behavior and unrealistic goals.

Calories—It can be helpful to expose nutritional myths, but discussions about the calorie content of food are usually unnecessary, unhelpful, and often harmful. Commit to eliminating calorie talk from your self talk or communication with others.

Diets—Talking about hunger is fine. Refrain from focusing on restrictive eating as a personal triumph or goal.

Perfection—In general, perfection is an unrealistic and destructive goal. (See Session 6.) Many who struggle with food issues are trapped in striving for perfection. Instead, encourage all people to appreciate themselves and their accomplishments however imperfect they may be.

Conformity—If everyone constantly tried to conform to current societal norms and expectations about body weight and appearance, the epidemic of eating disorders would be even larger than it is. Choose to listen to your own values and make decisions based on your position in Christ rather than conformity to the world.

Criticism—When you recognize a problem and identify a possible solution, feel free to offer it. However, stress that you are offering a suggestion, not a criticism. Focus on choices. Be cautious about judgments. Focus on affirmation.

Summarize your choices for change.

Personal response.

I am choosing to change my focus in the following ways:

Personal response.

Each group member is encouraged to:

Update goal for the week regarding eating behaviors or thought patterns

and/or

Set a goal related to "freedom from sociocultural influences."

Closing Prayer

Share updated prayer requests. After praying for the requests, thank God for what He is doing in the life of each group member.

Session 6 Letting Go of Perfectionism

Introduction

Allow 10 Minutes

Opening Prayer

Thank God that in our struggles, He loves and receives us where we are. Thank Him for helping us to become all that He has planned for our lives.

Sharing Question

What was the most challenging thing for you this week?

or

What have you learned about yourself this week?

Personal response.

The feminine pronoun is used in the text; however, males are also subject to eating disorders and the percentages are gradually increasing.

Self-Awareness

Allow 20 – 25 Minutes

Perfectionism leads to unrealistic and unattainable expectations of ourselves. (Look back at the "Lies We Believe" self-analysis questionnaire in Session 2.) Perhaps it is no coincidence that Chris Thurman lists "I must be perfect" as the first "self lie." The need to be perfect truly is a "self lie." Does scripture address perfectionism? Definitely! God requires perfectionism (theologically translated as "righteousness") for us to be in relationship with Him. As our Creator, He knew we would never be able to attain this perfectionism. (Adam and Eve made sure of that!) "There is no one righteous, not even one" (Romans 3:10). God instead provided the means for the perfectionism He requires through the death and resurrection of the only One who has ever attained perfection—our Lord and Savior, Jesus Christ.

The whole flow of the Bible is the story of God working mightily through imperfect men and women.

Christ died for me:
- Because I cannot be perfect.
- So that I need not be perfect.

Perfectionism is not only a nonbeliever's issue however. Even Christians who have solved the theological perfectionism dilemma battle perfectionism. Having extreme rules and definitions by which we measure ourselves leads to exquisite torment. When nearly everything attempted is evaluated as failure, feelings of inadequacy and worthlessness develop and grow.

Perfectionism wears two faces:

Even when I do something 99.9 percent perfect, I am still defective because there is the .1 percent imperfection I missed.

What fear does this face represent?

Fear of failure.

Since I cannot possibly do *it* right (i.e., 100 percent), I will not do it at all.

What opposite fear does this second face represent?

Fear of success.

Each of our unreasonable perfectionistic expectations is based on a false belief or "cognitive distortion." Each must be identified and then reframed to eliminate the irrational and illogical aspects of the thoughts, feelings, and actions.

"Perfectionism" is the bridge between the eating-disordered characteristics:
- control

  and
- low self-esteem/lack of identity

If I lack a sense of identity, I tend to feel "out of control"; perfectionism is my desperate attempt to establish control which I falsely expect will give me "identity."

Two major irrational beliefs that lead to attempts at perfectionism are:

- ***Conditional love***

"I won't be loved unless I am perfect."
(This belief comes from a society and/or family which determines value by performance and achievement as measured

by salary, bank accounts, popularity, grades, and other people's opinions of you.

- ***Black and white thinking***
  "If I'm not getting straight A's in school, I might as well get straight F's."

  "If I can't please everyone, I must not be pleasing anyone."

  "If I overeat at this meal, I'll overeat at every meal."

  Do you consider yourself a perfectionist? Why or why not?

Personal response.

Complete the following checklist to substantiate or refute your answer.

Checking as few as 3 of these statements places you at risk for perfectionism.

How Do I Score as a Perfectionist?

Check any of the following which describe you:

___ 1. Because of fear, I often avoid participating in certain activities.
___ 2. When I sense I might experience failure in some important area, I become nervous and anxious.
___ 3. I worry.
___ 4. I have unexplained anxiety.
___ 5. I am rarely satisfied with the quality of my work.
___ 6. I am compelled to justify my mistakes.
___ 7. There are certain areas in which I feel I must succeed.
___ 8. I become depressed when I fail.
___ 9. I become angry with people who interfere with my attempts to succeed and, as a result, make me appear incompetent.
___ 10. I am self-critical.

So, **are** you a perfectionist?

Personal response.

Spiritual Awareness Lead-In

Jesus says, "Be perfect, therefore, as your heavenly Father is perfect" (Matthew 5:48). At first glance, this passage seems impossible. However, perfect does not mean sinless but that the focus is on a close relationship with God. Our heavenly Father is not the example because He is sinless (though He is) but because He is our model of ultimate love. Our goal is a Christlike life.

Spiritual-Awareness

Allow 20-25 Minutes

Which perfectionist *face* do you wear? Refer back to the face of perfectionism. (Fear of Failure or Fear of Success.)

Let's take a look at what the Word of God has to say about *perfectionism.*

Ephesians 2:8-9
According to this passage, why is our salvation not dependent on performance?

Salvation is a gift received by grace through faith; it is not based on performance (works).

Philippians 1:6
Who is the author and completor of our perfect state?

Jesus Christ.

2 Corinthians 3:4-5
Where does true competence come from?

God.

Philippians 3:10-14
What were the Apostle Paul's performance goals?

Paul's desire was to KNOW Christ. To do so, he forgot the past and pressed "on toward the goal to win the prize" (v14).

Philippians 4:13
Does this verse imply that we are capable of perfection? Why or why not? (Note verses 11-12.)

No. The "all things" we can do are to be those things God wills for us to do. This also gives us contentment whatever our circumstances.

What do the following verses tell us are our performance responsibilities?

Psalm 84:5-7

We are to obtain our strength from our relationship with the Lord and to allow our lives to be a "pilgrimage" of growing stronger in Him throughout each of our challenges.

Hebrews 12:1-2

We are to rid ourselves of any sin and anything that hinders us from fixing our eyes on Jesus (i.e., no false gods and no idols).

Hebrews 6:11-12

Be diligent and "imitate those who through faith and patience (not performance) inherit what has been promised."

Micah 7:7-8

"Watch in hope for the Lord."

Philippians 4:6-7

We are never to be anxious but instead to make our requests known through prayer with a thankful heart.

Application

Allow 20 Minutes

Self-Perception and Perfectionism

We develop our self-perception by noticing how the important people in our life see us. If we grew up in a dysfunctional family, their skewed view of us probably warped our ability to see ourselves as we truly are in God's eyes. Understanding how God sees us and the value He has placed on us can help us over the negative self-perceptions many of us have developed.

God demonstrates to us how much He truly values us in that He considered us worthy enough to give up His only Son for us.

When we measure ourselves by those around us or by our own need to be perfect, we may not even try to succeed. All God asks is that we try to do something with our abilities and resources. When we allow ourselves the option of just making moderate progress (baby steps), we will find the courage to progress in our recovery and in life.

If I find myself stifled by my own insecurities of what others think of me and of what I am unwilling to express, I tend to forget what God thinks of me and instead get caught in:

— But God, I can't ...
— What if I fail ...
— What if I can't do it well enough for his/her/their expectations ...

Read Psalm 32:3-7. What does King David's example encourage us to do?

To acknowledge our sin and not cover up our iniquity. We are told that God is "my hiding place. You will protect me from trouble" (v7).

Who do you see as important enough to influence your self-perception? Is your perception balanced?

Personal response.

Where do you find your reach for perfectionism getting in your way?

Personal response.

What opportunities do you let get away because you cannot do them "well enough"?

Personal response.

God wants us to be successful. Biblical success and well-being are achieved by *becoming the me God has made me to be.* (We can actually be *the best* in something and miss what God's best for us is!) Biblically we are encouraged to have an accurate picture of ourselves (Romans 12:3). Success is being who I am—over the long haul.

Prepared by Betsy Hartley. Betsy is a "charter member" of the author's own support group and prepared this devotional application as part of her role as group co-facilitator.

How do you define success? Is your definition biblical? If not, what will it take for you to move from a worldly view to a biblical view of success?

Personal response.

Christian psychiatrist Dr. Raymond Vath's *Rules for Living* are:

1. If it's worth doing, it's worth doing even poorly.
2. Practice makes better, not perfect.
3. It is better to try and fail than to fail by not trying.
4. We should fail at half the things we try in life, or we will never know what we are capable of accomplishing (p. 92).

Pick one(or more) of Dr. Vath's *Rules* to implement in your life this week.

Suggestions for *Changing Perfectionistic Behavior:*

- Instead of seeing *the glass of life* as half empty or half full, begin to see it as both half empty and half full as well as all gradations in between. Acknowledge life as *gracefully* wonderful.

- Test everything and hold onto that which proves to be true and good (1 Thessalonians 5:21).

- Stop allowing the insignificant things in life to destroy your joy.

Each group member is encouraged to:

Adapt the following group goal for this week:
Pursue *competence,* not *superiority* (Alfred Adler).

Set a specific goal regarding *perfectionism.*

Closing Prayer

Share updated prayer requests. Thank God for the faithfulness of each group member. Thank Him for loving us with an unconditional love.

Session 7 Low Self-Esteem: A Christian Oxymoron

Introduction

Allow 10 Minutes

Opening Prayer

Thank God for allowing us to know Him and fellowship with Him. Pray that we may see ourselves as being "in Christ."

Sharing Question

How do you feel today?

or

The major obstacle you faced this week was . . .

Personal response.

Example: Thoughts of giving up, tempted to purge, fuss with mother, etc.

Self-Awareness

Allow 20-25 Minutes

In this session we address low self-esteem, both as one of the ten major emotional/perceptual triggers for development of an eating disorder and also as an *oxymoron* for the Christian. (Oxymoron: a figure of speech in which incongruous or contradictory terms are combined.)

While the Bible encourages us not to think more highly of ourselves than we ought (Romans 12:3) and commands us to look out not only for our own interests but also for the interests of others (Philippians 2:4), nowhere in the Bible are we told to put ourselves down. Bob Moorehead in the "Inferiority" chapter of *Counsel Yourself and Others From the Bible* lists seven common causes of inferiority feelings (pp. 192-194):

1. Less than ideal physical stature and appearance.
2. Academic limitations.
3. Vocational and economical factors.
4. Negative comparisons made by one's parents.
5. Poor health.
6. Criticism of others.
7. Satanic oppression.

These factors are but a paraphrase of the sociocultural factors we addressed in Session 5. Satan indeed uses sociocultural factors to oppress and keep us from expressing who we are in Christ.

For the Christian, low self-esteem (inferiority) is indeed an "oxymoron." Why? As Christians, we are called and privileged to lead a *God-centered* life rather than a *self-centered* life. Living a God-centered life brings self-esteem rather than self-centeredness. Author Don Matzat describes it as *Christ-Esteem.*

Below are the characteristics of the self-centered life and the God-centered life. Which characteristics from each list describe you?

Self-Centered

__ Life focused on self.
__ Proud of self and self accomplishments.
__ Self-confidence.
__ Depending on self and one's own abilities.
__ Affirming self.
__ Seeking to be acceptable to the world and its ways.
__ Looking at circumstances from a human perspective.
__ Selfish and ordinary living.

God-Centered

__ Confidence in God.
__ Dependence on God and His ability and provision.
__ Life focused on God and His activity.
__ Humble* before God.
*Biblical humility is defined as seeing oneself as God sees us.
__ Affirming God's work within self.
__ Seeking first the kingdom of God and His righteousness.
__ Holy and godly living.

Robert Frost in his famous poem, *The Road Less Travelled,* tells us about taking the "road less travelled" and how that has made all the difference.

Which road, *the self-centered life* or *the God-centered life,* do you think is analogous to Frost's less travelled road? Why?

Personal response.

How might traveling the God-centered road make *all the difference?*

Personal response.

Which road are you traveling? Which road do you want to travel?

Personal response.

Whom do you know who is following the God-centered road?

Personal response.

How is doing so making *all the difference* in their lives?

Personal response.

Spiritual Awareness Lead-In

The Apostle Paul shows the contrast between being self-centered and Christ-centered in Romans 7:24-25. In verse 24 he states, "What a wretched man I am! Who will rescue me from this body of death?" (self-centered). In verse 25 we see the focus on Christ. "Thanks be to God—through Jesus Christ our Lord!" (Christ-centered).

When we focus on self, we see emptiness. When we focus on Christ, there is cause for thankfulness.

Spiritual-Awareness

Allow 20-25 Minutes

The scriptures for Session 7 focus on God's positive view of us and benefits toward us. If we believe these scriptures, how can we possibly wear the mask of low self-esteem?

Matthew 3:17
What does God the Father's comment to God the Son at His baptism tell us about what God's love for us is and is not based upon?

God referred to Jesus as His beloved Son. Christ had yet to begin His ministry. His Father's love was based on His being a child of God, as are we, not on anything Jesus had "done" (i.e., not on performance).

Genesis 1:27
What does this verse tell us about ourselves which demands that we take captive any thoughts of low self-esteem?

Remember, we are created in ***God's image***!

Psalm 8:4-5
According to the psalmist, how does God view man and woman?

God made us only a little lower than the angels and crowned us with glory and honor.

Jeremiah 31:3
How long has God loved you?

He has loved us "with an ***everlasting*** love."

Facilitator's Guide: *Seeing Yourself in God's Image,* Turning Point, P. O. Box 22127, Chattanooga, TN 37422-2127

Zephaniah 3:17
In addition to loving us, what does God promise?

He promises to be with us, to save us from the world's destruction, to take great delight in us, to quiet us with His love, and to rejoice over us.

1 Peter 2:9
As the body of Christ, what "status" do we hold and why?

We are a chosen people, a royal priesthood, a holy nation, a people belonging to God so that we may declare the praises of God who called us from darkness to light.

Galatians 2:20
What does this verse tell us about the power source of our lives?

Christ living in me (I personally am crucified).

2 Peter 1:3a
What is the source of everything we need for life?

God's divine power.

Application

Allow 20 Minutes

In addition to giving us seven causes of inferiority feelings, Bob Moorehead in *Counsel Yourself and Others from the Bible* (pp. 194-199) also gives us six steps of counsel from God's Word to help combat inferiority:

First, realize you are in good company! Although many biblical characters struggled with low self-esteem, God used them in great ways.

Understand our sense of well-being is not derived from what we have but who we are in Christ.

Remember, God uses ordinary people in extraordinary ways.

Remember, our *goal* is to *please God*, not man.

Recognize that whatever we accomplish, we do so by God's strength.

Let Christ live His life through you.

Let's continue our *travelled road* metaphor from the Self-Awareness section. God created us with the need to belong and to contribute. Following are two diagrams. The first depicts what often happens and the second what can happen.

Which diagram best represents the road you are currently traveling? Why?

Personal response.

Diagram 1:

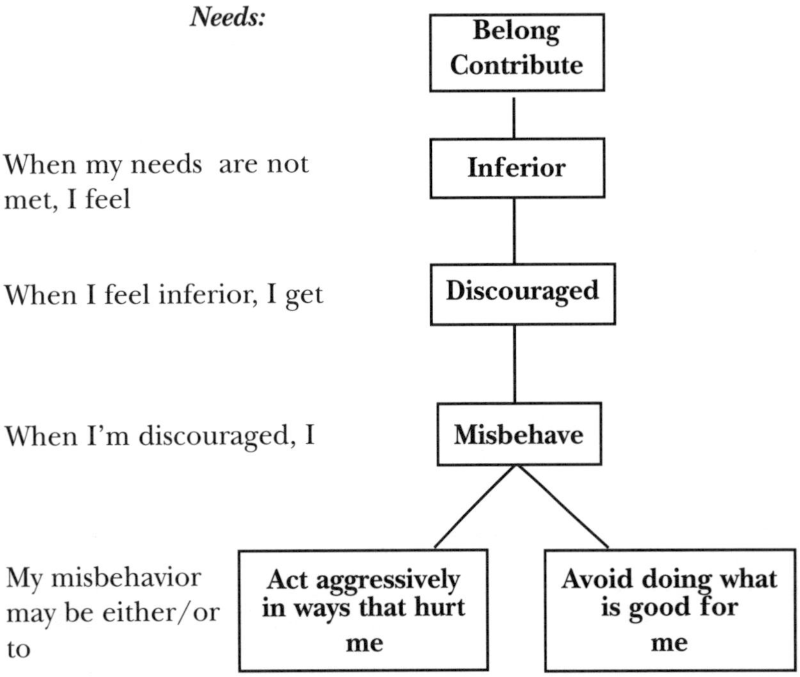

Diagram 2:

When I make truthful, healthy choices, I

When I behave, I feel

When I am encouraged, I experience

When I experience self-esteem, I also

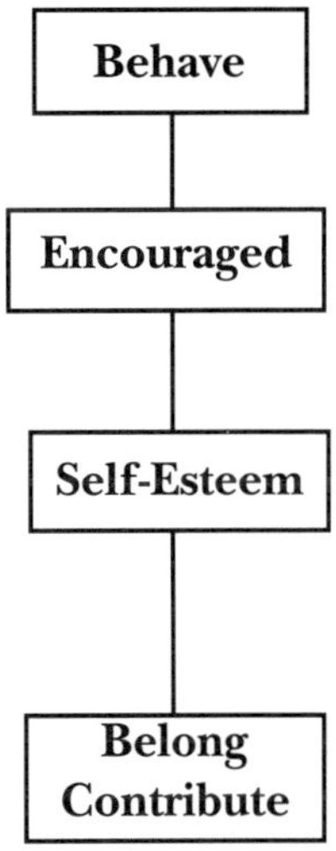

Remember the *baby steps* to recovery in Session 6 (Application)? Below is a poem to help you evaluate your progress: (Stanza III is a place to strive for in moving toward recovery; do not view your recovery in *black and white* terms.)

I

I walk down the street.
There is a deep hole in the sidewalk.
I fall in.
I am lost—I am helpless.
It isn't my fault.
It takes forever to find a way out.

II

I walk down the same street.
There is a deep hole in the sidewalk.
I pretend I don't see it.
I fall in again.
I can't believe I'm in the same place.
But it isn't my fault.
It still takes a long time to get out.

III

I walk down the same street.
There is a deep hole in the sidewalk.
I see it is there.
I still fall in—it's a habit.
My eyes are open.
I know where I am.
It is my fault.
I get out immediately.

IV

I walk down the same street.
There is a deep hole in the sidewalk.
I walk around it.

V

I walk down another street.

Author Unknown

Practice using either of the following tools to begin to take charge of any feelings of low self-esteem:

Apply the ***Truth*** system from Session 2. Identify a *triggering event* which has fed feelings of low self-esteem. What reckless thinking is leading to these feelings? What truthful thinking will you use to replace the reckless thinking? (Be specific.)

Encourage at least one group member to model each of these tools during this group sharing time as time permits.

The Four Key Questions Tool

We are in charge of choosing healthy behaviors and feelings based on truthful thinking and pro-activity. Use the following questions to address *misbehavior* (aggression or avoidance):

What do I want?

Personal responses.

What am I doing?

Is it working?

Can I figure out a better way? If so, what?

Be encouraged to:

Adapt the famous Eleanor Roosevelt quote as an affirmation for the week: *Remember, no one can make you feel inferior without your consent.* (Author's addition—including Satan.)

Set a specific goal regarding godly self-esteem.

Closing Prayer

Ask the group to go around the circle and pray for the person on their right perhaps about something they heard during the group or something that is on their heart. It is okay for the prayer to be brief, even one sentence. If anyone feels uncomfortable doing this she can say pass. The facilitator should conclude the prayer. Continue to remember prayer requests.

Session 8 Expression of the Depression: Living Out Loud

Introduction

Allow 10 Minutes

Opening Prayer

Thank God for each member present, for bringing them back again, and for touching their lives with His love. Pray that faith in God will help each one who is dealing with depression.

Sharing Questions

On a scale of 1-10 (10 high), how was your ED (eating disorder) recovery this week? Explain.

Personal response.

What support/accountability do you need from the group regarding this challenge?

Personal response.

Self-Awareness

Allow 20 – 25 Minutes

Depression is practically a household word. Since it means different things to different people, let's start this section with a working definition. Drs. Les Carter and Frank Minirth in *The Freedom from Depression Workbook* define depression as a "feeling of sadness and dejection resulting in an increasingly pessimistic outlook on life" (p. 7).

Depression often manifests itself in poor concentration and a breakdown in reasoning abilities. It is usually accompanied by such symptoms as social withdrawal, decreased motivation, lessened sexual desire, sleep disturbances, increased anxiety, edginess, and/or critical thoughts.

Depression is worsened by an ongoing habit of suppressing emotions and is often generated by the lack of emotional expression. (A common "lay" definition of depression is: "anger turned inward.") The opposite of depression is indeed "expression." Hence, an antidote for depression is often the encouragement to "Live Out Loud."

What triggers depression? Brenda Poinsett in *Why Do I Feel This Way?* (pp. 39-45) identifies the following triggers:

- Stressful Events
- Loss
- Chronic Stress
- Overload
- Unrealistic Expectations
- Pursuit of Thinness*
- Lack of Meaning
- No Control
- Unexpressed Emotions

*Pursuit of thinness is listed as a trigger on its own because this one trigger has been used as a major explanation for the difference in the depression rate of men and women. Both the pursuit of thinness and the thinness itself fuel depression (a side effect of starvation is depression).

If we look back at the emotional and perceptual characteristics of the eating-disordered personality (Session 1) which we are addressing in these 13 sessions, we see how enmeshed, entwined, and entangled they are with these "depression triggers":

Emotional Characteristic	**Related Depression Trigger**
Distorted Body Image	Pursuit of Thinness
Reckless Thinking	Unrealistic Expectations
Perfectionism	Unrealistic Expectations
Low Self-Esteem	Unrealistic Expectations
Depression	
• Masked Anger	Unexpressed Emotions
• Unresolved Grief	Loss
Control	No Control
Dependency	Stressful Events
Sexual Identity	Stressful Events
Family System's Influence	Stressful Events
	Chronic Stress
	Overload
	Lack of Meaning
Sociocultural Influence	Stressful Events
	Chronic Stress
	Overload
	Lack of Meaning

When we realize how enmeshed, entwined, and entangled all of the eating-disordered characteristics are, is it any wonder that the eating-disordered individual and/or her family begins to feel helpless and hopeless!

Do you consider yourself depressed?

Personal response.

If so, which of the symptoms of depression (described in the first part of Self-Awareness) are you experiencing?

Personal response.

What triggers (triggered) the depression? (Did your depression trigger the eating disorder or did the eating disorder trigger the depression? (Explain.)

Personal response.

Depression often presents itself as:

- Masked Anger
  and/or
- Unresolved Grief

Which of these categories best describes your depression? Explain.

Personal response.

Spiritual Awareness Lead–In

Depression often leads to isolation. "Encourage one another daily, as long as it is called Today, so that none of you may be hardened by sin's deceitfulness" (Hebrews 3:13). Encouraging one another helps to break down the walls of isolation. By doing so, we can prevent or deal with hardness of heart and the delusion of sin.

Spiritual-Awareness

Allow 20–25 Minutes

How does the Word of God respond to depression which is triggered by each of the following:

Isaiah 43:2-3
Stressful Events

No matter what the circumstances we are experiencing, God will be with us.

Psalm 147:3; 2 Corinthians 1:3; Matthew 5:4
Loss

The Lord heals the brokenhearted and binds their wounds. The Father of compassion and the God of all comfort comforts us in all our troubles. Those who mourn shall be comforted.

2 Corinthians 4:16-17 Chronic Stress	We are not to lose heart even though we are confronted with chronic stressors. If we walk closely with the Lord, we will be renewed inwardly daily; the troubles of the present are "achieving for us an eternal glory" (v17).
1 Kings 19:3-13 Overload	Elijah was crashing after two great spiritual victories. To lead him out of the depression, God first encouraged him to rest and eat. Then He reminded him to return to his mission rather than stay "down on himself."
2 Corinthians 10:5; Romans 12:2 Unrealistic Expectations	Unrealistic expectations are managed best by taking every thought captive for Christ (What Would Jesus Do?) and by renewing our minds with right thinking.
3 John 2 Pursuit of Thinness	God is concerned about our physical health as well as our spiritual well-being.
Jeremiah 29:11 Lack of Meaning	The Lord has a positive plan for each of our lives.
Proverbs 3:5-8 No Control	Trusting in the Lord provides biblical control and wisdom (makes our paths straight).
Psalm 32:3 Unexpressed Emotions (including sins)	Unexpressed emotion and sin cause us to waste away physically, emotionally, and spiritually.

Steps to Managing Depression

1. Be aware of key indicators that "expression" is needed.
   - Recognize the symptoms.
   - Identify the triggers.

2. If you are masking anger, acknowledge it, identify its purpose, and make choices for defusing it.

3. Ask the Lord to help you identify unresolved losses. Seek His guidance for healthy ways to grieve these losses.

4. Commit to healthy boundaries to:
   - Foster realistic expectations.
   - Prevent overload.
   - Minimize stressful events and chronic stress.

5. Believe in yourself. Know you are a worthwhile and valuable person.

6. Refuse to perpetuate or tolerate any present or past abuse.

7. Recognize how your personality and genetic makeup can predispose you to depression.

8. Investigate psychopharmaceutical intervention in the management of the depression.

9. Commit to positive attitudes that can bring balance to your feelings and emotions.

Which of the above suggestions will you commit to?

Personal responses.

Purging Feelings

The opposite of depression is expression. In this activity, we will be given an opportunity to express feelings and emotions that are feeding our eating disorders. This will be a *healthy* purge!

Provide several packets of post-it notes and a whiteboard. On the whiteboard, draw a large cross.

Refer to the *feelings list* at the end of this section. Identify your heaviest, unexpressed feelings. Write these feelings on post-it notes, one feeling per post-it note.

Which of these feelings are you ready to take to the cross and let Jesus Christ free you of or carry for you?

Personal response.

After each group member has completed the question, take turns sharing with the group:

The feelings you identified

Why/how they are feeding your eating disorder

Select at least one of these feelings to take to the cross. (Place the post-it note on which you have written that feeling on the cross provided for this session.) Ask Jesus to take that feeling for you. As you do so, let go of the power that feeling has had over you.

Each group member is encouraged to:

Adapt the following group goal for this week:
Express; Don't Depress. Choose to *Live Out Loud.*

Set a specific goal regarding depression management.

Closing Prayer

Continue to remember the prayer requests. Give time for group members to share a prayer and then close with the final prayer.

Physically oriented

alert
alive
aroused
beat
breathless
cold
comfortable
energetic
enervated
enlivened
excited
exhausted
exhilarated
famished
fatigued
full
gorged
hot
hungry
hurt
ill
invigorated
jittery
lethargic
listless
nervous
refreshed
relaxed
restless
run-down
rushed
shaky
sick
sleepy
steady
stiff
strong
tense
tired
titillated
uncomfortable
unsteady
warm
weak
weary
well
wide-awake
worn

Slang

beat
blah
blue
brokenhearted
burned out
charged
down
edgy
electrified
great
grossed out
groovy
hacked off
hepped up
high
hot
in touch
keyed up
loose
mellow
messed up
miffed
mopey
off
on
on edge
out of it
pooped
psyched
psyched up
run-down
rushed
shot
spent
teed off
ticked off
tight
together
turned off
turned on
under the weather
undone
unglued
unhinged
up
uptight
wasted
whipped
wiped out
wired
with it
zapped
zonked
out of touch

Spiritually oriented

alive
apathetic
awakened
bad
bored
bound
committed
complacent
confident
courageous
dead
defeated
despairing
detached
discouraged
disheartened
dissatisfied
downhearted
empty
enlightened
enlivened
fearful
free
fulfilled
full
good
guilty
helpless
hopeful
hopeless
indifferent
insecure
inspired
joyful
joyous
jubilant
lonely
lost
loving
moved
optimistic
overwhelmed
peaceful
penitent
pessimistic
powerful
powerless
proud
redeemed
renewed
repentant
satisfied
secure
strong
sure
thankful
touched
trustful
unsure
whole

Cognitively oriented

absorbed
alert
amazed
ambivalent
appreciative
complacent
composed
concerned
confused
curious
engrossed
fascinated
hesitant
inquisitive
interested
intrigued
involved
optimistic
perplexed
puzzled
reluctant
skeptical
stimulated
suspicious
unconcerned
uninterested
unnerved

Emotionally oriented

afraid
aggravated
agitated
alarmed
amused
angry
annoyed
anxious
apprehensive
aroused
astonished
bad
bitter
calm
comfortable
concerned
confused
contented
cross
dejected
delighted
depressed
disappointed
discouraged
disgruntled
disgusted
dismayed
displeased
distressed
distraught
disturbed
downcast
downhearted
ecstatic
elated
electrified
embarrassed
enthralled
exhilarated
frightened
frustrated
furious
glad
grateful
grieved
happy
horrified
hurt
infuriated
irked
irritated
jealous
jittery
joyful
joyous
jubilant
lonely
mad
melancholic
merry
miserable
mortified
nettled
overjoyed
pleased
rancorous
relieved
resentful
sad
scared
shocked
sorrowful
spellbound
splendid
surprised
taken back
tense
terrified
touched
tranquil
troubled
undone
uneasy
unhappy
upset
vexed

Session 9 Who/What Is in Control?

Introduction

Allow 10 Minutes

Opening Prayer

Thank God for the faithfulness of each group member. Thank Him for the privilege of belonging to one another in a caring community of believers in Jesus Christ.

Sharing Questions

What was the major obstacle in your recovery this week? Explain.

Personal response.

What support/accountability do you need from the group regarding this challenge?

Personal response.

Self-Awareness

Allow 20–25 Minutes

Anorexia and bulimia are *diseases* of control. There is dis-*ease* with the degree of control in one's emotional, psychological, and spiritual life as well as with one's family and sociocultural influences. To cope and to hopefully gain some semblance of control, the individual *attempts* to control her physical self. ("The only place I can take charge is with what I eat!" The anorexic consequently restricts her food intake. For the bulimic, the binge is a picture of her lack of control which she attempts to regain by purging.)

Eating-disordered individuals use food to give a false sense of control. The "thin" outside gives a pretense to themselves and others of being internally "in control." In truth, internally their emotions, their spirituality, and their thinking are severely out of control.

Eating disordered control issues involve both:

Who's in control
and
What's in control.

Facilitator's Guide: *Seeing Yourself in God's Image*, Turning Point, P. O. Box 22127, Chattanooga, TN 37422-2127

Who's in control? Satan has convinced us that we can, we ought to be in control of our lives. The truth is that God is and ought to be in control. The first step to gaining appropriate control is to acknowledge this freeing fact: "If God is for us, who can be against us?" (Romans 8:31b).

What's in control? The question might better be asked as *What do we allow to control us?* Is it anger, fear, lies, family, or sociocultural influences? When we allow the *Who's in Control* to be God, we are also reminded that "God did not give us a spirit of timidity, but a spirit of power, of love and of self-discipline" (2 Timothy 1:7). This empowerment by God allows us, encourages us, and expects us to *take charge* of the influences that weigh us down and not give that control to food.

Belongingness and contribution are basic God-given human needs (refer back to Application in Session 7). According to psychiatrist Alfred Adler, dysfunctional individuals gain a sense of belonging by employing one of four personality priorities:

Pleasing
Control
Comfort
Superiority

The two personality priorities usually adopted by the eating disordered are pleasing and control.

PLEASERS strive to belong by achieving success in relationships. They are friendly, keep the peace, anxious to please, and are noncompetitive.

They *avoid* rejection and anger.

They hide negative feelings to avoid rejection and battle with food rather than people (i.e., they stuff or restrict food and feelings).

CONTROLLERS strive to belong by controlling others or maintaining maximum self-control. (The eating-disordered individual usually adopts the latter.)

They *avoid* feelings of powerlessness, being out of control, humiliation, and embarrassment. Their perceived lack of control leads to control of their own body.

Adler also addresses the major *Life Tasks*:

Friendship and Love
Self
Work
Spirituality (Added later by students of Adler)

The eating-disordered individual's dysfunctional behavior in these life tasks include:

Friendship and Love—Overtly manages relationships yet fears intimacy and isolates oneself.

Self—Poor self-esteem, very self-critical.

Work—Overachieving and overambitious.

Spirituality—*Control* needs are in conflict with the faith concept. Faith issues are frequently ignored because the eating disordered individual is so busy trying to please others, stay in control, and be perfect they allow little time and energy for pursuing spiritual growth.

Which of the "personality priorities" best describes you? Explain.

Personal response.

In which of the *life tasks* is your eating disorder creating the most difficulty? Why?

Personal response.

Spiritual Awareness Lead-In

Romans 8:6 and 8:8 provide a contrast in control. Describe the two.

"The mind controlled by the Spirit is life and peace" (v6).

"Those controlled by the sinful nature cannot please God" (v8).

Who is in control?

What do the following verses tell us about the benefits of allowing God to be in control of our lives?

Proverbs 3:5-8

If I trust in the Lord and lean on Him and not on my own understanding and wisdom (or lack of understanding and wisdom) plus shun evil (i.e., reject Satan and his influences in my life), God will make my paths straight (provide appropriate "control") and bring health to my body and "nourishment to [my] bones."

Psalm 18:1-3; 16-21; 28

The Lord is my strength, my rock, my fortress, my deliverer, my shield. He saves me from my enemies (including myself). He reaches down and takes hold of me to draw me out of deep waters and rescues me from my powerful enemy, from my foes who are too strong for me. He is my support, and He turns my darkness into light.

Philippians 4:6-7

If we are not anxious but pray with thanksgiving, the peace of God will guard our hearts and our minds.

2 Corinthians 11:14
Why do we need to be very cautious whom we listen to and who our role models are?

Satan masquerades as an angel of light and will attempt to destroy us.

What is in control?

Luke 8:1-15 (Note verses 7 and 14 specifically.)
What does the parable of the sower teach us about the development of an eating disorder?

Even though the seeds of the Word of God may have been planted in our lives, if we allow thorns to grow up (life's worries, riches, pleasures—translated as sociocultural and family influences, perfectionism, distorted body image, reckless thinking, etc.), the Word will be choked and we will "starve."

Romans 13:14
What does this verse encourage us to do?

Clothe ourselves with Christ "and do not think about how to gratify the desires of the sinful nature" (i.e., the world's standards of happiness).

Hebrews 12:1-6
How do we keep the *who* and *what* under appropriate control?

We are to identify and throw off every sin that so easily entangles us and run with perseverance the race Christ has set before us, fixing our eyes on Him.

2 Corinthians 10:5
But how?

By taking every thought captive for Christ (i.e., WWJT—What Would Jesus Think).

Philippians 4:13
From where does my true strength to do this come?

I can do all things through **Christ** who strengthens me (i.e., all He wants me to do). By allowing Him to be in control of my life, I will have the strength to do the important and right things.

Application

Allow 20 Minutes

Complete as many of the following *control-related* activities as time permits.

Two Types of Control

Controllers have precise definitions of right and wrong and in order to *color within those lines* either strive to control others or maintain maximum self-control.

Two types of control are necessary in order to cover all control bases:

Offensive control—acting upon life and those around us.
Defensive control—protecting ourselves from being acted upon.

The lies we believe are a form of *control.* Refer again to *The Lies We Believe* from Session 2 and identify the **offensive** lies with an "O" and the **defensive** lies with a "D."

Discuss with the group by comparing your answers. Group responses will vary.

SELF LIES
___ 1. I must be perfect.
___ 2. I must have everyone's love and approval.
___ 3. It is easier to avoid problems than to face them.
___ 4. Things have to go my way for me to be happy.
___ 5. My unhappiness is externally caused.

WORLDLY LIES
___ 6. I can have it all.
___ 7. I am only as good as what I do.
___ 8. Life should be easy.
___ 9. Life should be fair.
___ 10. I shouldn't have to wait for what I want.
___ 11. People are basically good.

MARRIAGE LIES

___ 12. My marriage problems are my spouse's fault.

___ 13. If my marriage takes hard work, my spouse and I must not be right for each other.

___ 14. My spouse should meet all my needs.

___ 15. My spouse owes me for what I have done for him/her.

___ 16. I shouldn't have to change who I am in order to make my marriage better.

___ 17. My spouse should be like me.

DISTORTION LIES

___ 18. I often make mountains out of molehills.

___ 19. I often take things personally.

___ 20. Things are black and white to me.

___ 21 I often miss the forest for the trees.

___ 22. The past predicts the future.

___ 23. I often reason things out with my feelings rather than with the facts.

.

RELIGIOUS LIES

___ 24. God's love can be earned.

___ 25. God hates the sin and the sinner.

___ 26. Because I'm a Christian, God will protect me from pain and suffering.

___ 27. All of my problems are caused by my sins.

___ 28. It is my Christian duty to meet all the needs of others.

___ 29. Painful emotions such as anger, depression, and anxiety are signs that my faith in God is weak.

___ 30. God can't use me unless I am spiritually strong.

The Lies We Believe Workbook by Chris Thurman, Thomas Nelson, 1995, pp. 3-4. Used with permission. (Section headings added.)

In *The Circles of Love: A Map to Wellness*, Marcia Thompson, M.Ed., M.S.E., refers to two postures which keep us from making adult choices—the wounded posture which is reflected in shame and the warrior posture which protects itself through control.

Which posture best describes you? Explain.

Personal response.

What support/accountability do you need in order to move from the wounded or warrior posture to a *choice-making* adult posture?

Personal response.

Decoding Body Messages

An initial goal of all eating disorder therapies is to help the client *decode* their negative talk about their bodies and understand the function the coding serves. Following is an example of decoding:

> Ann realizes that whenever she feels *hungry* for people or food, she feels *out of control* and hopeless about getting her needs met. She looks in the mirror, sees herself as fat, believes that fatness is the cause of her hopelessness, and experiences a distortion of her body image. Her focus switches to changing her body, an attempt to focus on something concrete (her body) that she can effectively control. She has converted helplessness into action.

How does this example illustrate *coding*? Ann has *coded* her dual hunger both for food and people under food only. By ignoring her hunger for people (by her lack of confidence that she can feed that hunger), she *distorts* (codes) her need in a distorted body image which she attempts to bring back down to size via restricting or overexercising.

With the encouragement of her therapist (or support group), Ann begins to *ask for* the people interaction (people food) she is hungry for. This begins the *decoding* process, and she regains appropriate *control* as she separates food hunger from people hunger.

How do you use *coding* to attain false control?

Discuss this decoding example as a group.

What support/accountability do you need to *decode*?

Reclaiming Healthy Control

If you are struggling with *restrictive* eating patterns, experiment with the following questions to help you reclaim healthy control:

Encourage group members to experiment with the appropriate reminder questions during the week.

What do I get out of maintaining restrictive eating patterns?

What are the consequences of this choice?

What is driving me to restrict?

What will my eating pattern look like when I break the restriction?

If you are struggling with *binge/purge* eating patterns, experiment with the following questions to help you reclaim healthy control:

Can I take responsibility for this choice?

How will I feel after the ingestion?

Do I want this food to become a part of me?

How am I using this food—for physiological or psychological means? Restriction?

Each group member is encouraged to:

> Adapt the following **group goal** for this week: *I choose to give any control that is keeping me in bondage to any eating disordered behaviors back to God.*
>
> Set a specific goal regarding control management.

Closing Prayer

Pray for the prayer requests presented. Ask a group member or ask for a volunteer to conclude this session in prayer.

Session **10** *All Grown Up and Not Wanting to Go (The Role of Dependency)*

Introduction

Allow 10 Minutes

Opening Prayer

Thank God for the ministry of group members to each other over the last few weeks. Thank Him for the interest and progress (whether great or small).

Sharing Questions

Did you have any particular preoccupation with food this week that you would like to process with the group? If so, what? What role did *control* play in this preoccupation?

Personal response.

What support/accountability do you need from the group regarding this challenge?

Personal response.

Self-Awareness

Allow 20-25 Minutes

According to Dr. Raymond Vath, author of *Counseling Those with Eating Disorders*:

> It is not surprising that a person who sees herself as a failure, with seemingly uncontrollable behaviors, would look to others for control yet resist control because she has been taught to value autonomy and freedom.
>
> This leads to a condition of hostile dependency which has been present, to varying degrees, in the clients with whom I have worked. (p. 173)

Dependency: *All Grown Up and Wanting to Go.* Isn't that what we all look forward to? Growing up and moving into adult roles and responsibilities. If you have experienced the benefits of growing up in a family which fosters movement through the developmental stages of childhood and adolescence in a healthy, sequential order, your answer will be *yes*. For the individual growing up in a dysfunctional family (Christian or non-Christian) the answer is often *no*.

The severely ill eating-disordered individual is afraid to grow up. She fears taking on adult responsibilities. (What if she handles them as poorly as she handles her own health.) The anorexic profile is a picture of attempting to arrest psychosocial development for fear of facing relationship development with boys. (Sometimes, but not always, this is the result of childhood or adolescent sexual abuse.) Her flat chest and lack of periods are a picture of psychosocial smallness.

The bulimic profile, in contrast, pictures women who are able to hold responsible jobs and/or attempt the stresses of other adult responsibilities (e.g., college, marriage, and families). Due to her masked tormentors, however, the bulimic's obvious or subtle behavior is aimed at encouraging someone else to take charge of the out-of-control aspects of her life. She may physically be "all grown up," but she is "dependent" on others for her survival.

This failure to emancipate is not always the eating-disordered individual's choice. Often her attempt to become independent is subtly undermined by her own family, and the illness is unconsciously being reinforced. Think back to the characteristics of the eating disordered family. Enmeshment, rigidity, overprotection, conflict avoidance/detouring, and an atmosphere of inconsistency and/or high expectations do not exactly foster independence. Indeed, these characteristics prohibit the individual from developing "skills for life" or a sense of mastery and competence.

Vath describes the Karpman Triangle, a three-positional, interactional pattern that helps to understand further the dependency cycle of the eating-disordered individual and family (p. 174). This three-positional, interactional pattern of persecutor—victim—rescuer serves to maintain hope that someone else will solve *the problem.* Following is an example to illustrate this pattern:

> In the attempt to provoke the family to control her abusive eating habits, the bulimic will often binge on foods reserved for a family food occasion. If food is set aside exclusively for the use of the bulimic, she will eat that and the family's (or roommate's) food as well. After a purge, the bulimic will leave a smelly bathroom. Kleptomania may begin. The bulimic is victimizing her family through persecutory behaviors.
>
> When the family retaliates with harsh, firm rules such as, "If you want to eat, you'll have to earn your own money," or when the family criticizes and condemns, they move into the role of persecutor, and the bulimic

wife or daughter becomes the victim. In this role, the bulimic (or anorexic) engages in self-punitive behaviors such as excessive exercise, restricting, and/or increased binging/purging. Her health deteriorates; the family, feeling guilty for their harshness, reverts to the role of rescuer, and the cycle begins again. Unfortunately, when the family attempts to rescue their victim daughter, they foster dependency by implying that they can take responsibility for her behavior. Sometimes the roles are split with the father being a critical persecutor, the mother being the protective rescuer, and the daughter floundering in confusion about which role to be in. (The daughter feels trapped in a scenario of being both punished and rewarded for the same behavior.)

What new insights have you gained from this information on dependency?

Personal response.

What role does dependency play in reinforcing your eating-disordered behavior(s)?

Personal response.

Spiritual Awareness Lead-In

Ephesians 5:21 proclaims neither independence nor codependency but interdependence: "Submit to one another out of reverence for Christ."

What insures proper boundaries in relationships?

Our submission to one another is in respect for Christ. Our relationships should show our dependence on Christ thus bringing His due respect.

Spiritual-Awareness

Allow 20-25 Minutes

Read the following scriptures and reflect on what God's Word says about dependence and independence.

Philippians 1:6; Proverbs 3:5-8
On whom are we to remain dependent forever? Why?

God. God began "a good work" in us, and it is He who will complete that good work. Trusting in Him allows Him to "make [our] paths straight" (Proverbs 3:6).

Hebrews 4:14b, 16
On what are we to be dependent?

Our faith. It gives us confidence to approach the throne of grace where we receive mercy and find grace to help us in our time of need (which is at all times for the believer as we live in a world which is ruled by the prince of darkness).

Ecclesiastes 3:1-8
How does this famous passage relate to dependence and independence?

There is a time in our life to be dependent, but we are to move on to independence.

1 Corinthians 13:11
What does this verse tell us about the contrast between childhood and adulthood?

Children talk, think, and reason like children. When we become adults, we are to put away childish things and take on adult responsibilities (adult talk, thoughts, and reasoning).

Hebrews 5:14-6:1
Why are we to move from a diet of milk to a diet of solid spiritual food?

Milk keeps us spiritual infants not acquainted with mature Christian principles. Solid spiritual food is required for the maturity which empowers us to distinguish good from evil.

Jeremiah 29:11
How does this promise from God encourage our independence?

Knowing God has a plan for my life, a plan to prosper me and not to harm me, gives me courage to "take a whack" at independence and adult responsibilities.

2 Timothy 1:7
How does God equip us for independence?

His Holy Spirit gives us power, love, and self-discipline.

Which of these verses speak loudest to you? Why?

Personal responses.

Application

Allow 20 Minutes

In the healing process, we learn to be more and more dependent upon Christ. In doing so, we gain an independence to stand on our own feet. However, we still need one another in the body of Christ, and we should always be aware of codependency. Codependency is defined as dependence on things outside of oneself and one's relationship with the Lord. Codependency is when we master another person's life or another person masters our life.

As we are dependent upon Christ, we also need to be aware of proper balance in human relationships. There are times when we may take independence to extremes. Following are some core issues through which you may need to work:

- All or nothing thinking and acting sharply and unrealistically limits possibilities and choices and restricts creativity; think in shades of gray instead.
- Control: The more I try to control, the more out of control I feel. Choose the alternative: surrender.
- Being overly responsible is a way to avoid painful feelings such as anger, fear, hurt, abandonment.
- Neglecting my needs.
- High tolerance for inappropriate behavior.
- Fear of abandonment.
- Difficulty handling and resolving conflict (we learn to avoid conflict whenever possible). Healing is built on discovering conflict after conflict and then working through each.

Anger is a major component in grieving and in the healing process. Since most of us have experienced a large number of ungrieved losses in our lives, working through them may take a long time.

- Become aware of our upset or concern.
- Experience it, including telling our story about it.
- Consider the possibility that we have a choice to stop suffering over it and then:
    Forgive.
    Let go of it.

On the other hand, we need each other to grieve the pain of any ungrieved losses or traumas in the presence of safe and supportive people (when we feel something, we decrease its power over us). We can help one another in supportive, Christ-centered groups and identify our ongoing spiritual, mental, physical, and spiritual needs.

Galatians 6:1-5 deals with restoration. Verse 2 says, "Carry each other's burdens, and in this way you will fulfill the law of Christ." Indeed, we are to bear one another's burdens, but how much do we carry? What are the boundaries? Verse 5 tells us "For each one should carry his own load." The point here is personal responsibility. Everyone is responsible to God for his or her behavior and who he or she is. In some things faced in life, we will stand independent but dependent upon God.

RESPONSIBILITY

What does responsibility mean to you?

Personal responses.

Is there one specific responsibility that frightens you?

What responsibilities do you consciously avoid?

What keeps you from accepting these responsibilities? Have you even faced them yet?

Are there any responsibilities you have taken on that are not necessary? If so, why? If you could take any one of them away, which one would it be?

Are you looking forward to being capable of handling more responsibilities? Why or why not?

Each group member is encouraged to:

Adapt the following group goal for this week: *Moving from **dependence** to **independence** is an expansive opportunity!*

Set a specific goal regarding dependence management.

Closing Prayer

Pray for the prayer requests. Ask God to help each group member be dependent upon Him, responsible for her behavior, and interdependent in the body of Christ.

Session 11 Fearfully and Wonderfully Made: Correcting Distorted Sexual Identity

Introduction

Allow 10 Minutes

Opening Prayer

Thank God for the faithfulness of each group member. Thank Him for the uniqueness of each person and the contributions each one has made to this group.

Sharing Questions

How are you "thinking" of yourself today? How are you using the TRUTH system (Session 2)? Is it working? Why? Why not?

Personal response.

What support/accountability do you need from the group regarding your thinking?

Personal response.

Self-Awareness

Allow 20-25 Minutes

Females in our culture are encouraged, even pressured, to adopt a wide range of roles: wife, mother, girlfriend, student, employee, boss, professional. Is it any wonder that our identity becomes confused or distorted? Specifically, what it means to be a sexual female in light of all of these potential and often concurrent roles confuses and often distorts our beautiful, God-given sexual identity. The Church, society, and, unfortunately, abusive life experiences further complicate our sexual identity.

Helen Bray-Garretson and Kaye Cook in *Chaotic Eating: A Guide to Recovery* address the false belief that *thin is sexy*:

> If we perceive that thin women are more beautiful than the average woman, it is easy to believe that they are more sexually attractive, more likely to be worth loving. We can't imagine a fat person having a fulfilling sex life or being a satisfying sexual partner. But the truth is that sexual attraction, as experienced within the context of a

loving, committed relationship (within marriage for the Christian) [emphasis added] has little to do with thinness. Thinness does not automatically lead to satisfying sexual relationships.

Women become easily confused about the connections between thinness, sexuality, and relationships. Some women say that their passion goes into their eating and there's nothing left over for their intimate partners. As one woman explained it, "I'm more likely to get the 'hots' for a hot fudge sundae than for my husband." Other women point out that so much energy goes into worrying about their eating and what people are thinking about their bodies that they just don't care much about anything else (pp. 90-91).

According to Raymond Vath, MD, in *Counseling Those With Eating Disorders* (p. 122), if the female's parents' marriage is dysfunctional and/or the father-daughter relationship impaired, it will be difficult for the daughter to develop healthy relationships with men. First, her own identity as a woman may be insecure, and she will relate from a position of uncertainty and insecurity. She may feel such fear of a relationship that men will be avoided. If she does approach a relationship, it will be with ambivalence. Many bulimic women seek out men to date whom they would never marry. This allows them to feel attractive yet avoids the need to reveal inadequacy that a committed, intimate relationship would require.

Also, an insecure woman will be unduly vulnerable if a romantic relationship ends. She will search for the cause of her painful self-doubts, grief, and despair. Often the "stopping-off place" is a belief that her beauty was not sufficient to hold the relationship together.

Furthermore, if the father and mother's relationship is strained, the father may encourage his daughter to become "daddy's little girl." Anorexia or bulimia may surface due to a father's unconscious wish that his daughter never grow up and become capable of leaving the family. Or if one parent dies, the eating disorder provides a continuing symbolic relationship between the surviving parent and the daughter: The grieving parent is comforted by the daughter; her eating disorder "freezes" her at the age of the parent's death assuring no further losses for the surviving parent.

Sometimes eating disorders begin in adolescence when a father becomes threatened by his thoughts of his daughter's becoming a beautiful woman. This awareness of the daughter's sexuality provokes so much guilt the father and daughter spend the balance of their relationship fighting which ensures that considerable distance is kept between them.

Studies to determine if sexual abuse is a risk factor for the development of eating disorders have been contradictory and controversial (Garner and Garfinkel, p. 394). There is somewhat more evidence to suggest that childhood sexual abuse shows a stronger relationship to bulimic symptoms than to restricting anorexic symptomatology although further study of this issue is needed (Ibid., p. 397). The presence of childhood sexual abuse does seem to increase the likelihood for the development of an eating disorder but does not predict the likelihood for a more severe eating disorder. Finally, the presence of childhood physical abuse predicts poor outcome of treatment, but it remains generally unclear whether the presence of sexual abuse or other traumas is significantly predictive of the outcome of standardized, traditional eating disorder treatments (Ibid, p. 400).

What new insights have you gained from this information on the distortion of sexual identity?

Personal responses.

How positive would you rate your sexual identity on a 1-10 point scale (10 high)? Explain.

What are the predominant factors which have contributed to the development of your sexual identity?

What role does sexual identity play in reinforcing your eating-disordered behavior(s)?

Anorexia and bulimia are often responses to sexual abuse. For the anorexic, the goal is **to stay small**. *If I just stay small enough, I won't appear sexually desirable, and no one will hurt me that way again.*

For the bulimic the message may be *I can't stomach the abuse any longer.*

What other messages might an eating disorder represent for the victim of sexual abuse?

Note: If you have been sexually abused, it is imperative that you seek professional support.

Spiritual Awareness Lead-In

The Apostle Paul writes that "you should avoid sexual immorality . . . each of you should learn to control his [or her] own body in a way that is holy and honorable" (1 Thessalonians 4:3-4).

Paul gives a reason for this statement. What is it?

It is God's will.

Spiritual-Awareness

Allow 20-25 Minutes

Review the following scriptures and note what God's Word says about sexuality.

Psalm 139:13-14a
How does David describe the human body?

He describes it as "fearfully and wonderfully made" (14).

Song of Solomon 7
Select biblical descriptions of the beauty of sexuality as described by King Solomon and his bride.

Examples:
"Your graceful legs are like jewels" (v1).
"Your navel is a rounded goblet" (v2).
"Your waist is a mound of wheat encircled by lilies" (v2).
"Your breasts are like two fawns, twins of a gazelle" (v3).
"Your neck is like an ivory tower" (v4).
"Your eyes are the pools of Heshbon" (v4).
"Your nose is like the tower of Lebanon" (v4).
"How beautiful you are and how pleasing" (v6).
"May your breasts be like the clusters of the vine" (v8).

Ephesians 5:31-32
What notes husband and wife oneness in these verses?

After uniting, "the two will become one flesh." Sexual expression is reserved for marriage. This marriage bond takes on an even greater need to be practiced respectfully as we read that marriage, the only biblically sanctioned setting for sexuality, is a picture of Christ and the Church.

Genesis 2:24-25
God is the creator of marriage. Sexual expressions within marriage eliminate a major emotional problem. What is it?

"They felt no shame" (v25).

Application

Allow 20 Minutes

In 1 Corinthians 12:12-31, the Apostle Paul gives attention to the diversity of unity of the human body when comparing it to the body of Christ. He places special emphasis on the less honorable parts (verse 23) to make a point concerning the less presentable in the body of Christ. As described, the human body is a magnificent creation of God, and this passage shows its importance by comparing it to the body of Christ.

1. Recognize that your body is like no other. There is no room for comparison. God has made it special, unique in its beauty. Affirm your acceptance of all the parts of your body. Pull out a full length mirror in privacy and watch yourself move, bending, stretching, squatting, tightening, and relaxing muscles all over your body.

2. When you have personal thoughts that reflect self-disgust, body hatred, criticism, or embarrassment at the way your body compares to other people's bodies remember that you are the creation of God.

3. Focus on the affirmation: *This is my body, and I cherish it. I am fearfully and wonderfully made. Thank you, God.*

Adapted from Helen Bray-Garretson and Kaye V. Cook, *Chaotic Eating*, p. 92. Used with permission.

Write a prayer centered on "I am fearfully and wonderfully made" (Psalm 139:14).

Ask for group members to share their prayers as time permits.

Set a specific goal regarding accepting and affirming your feminine sexual identity.

Closing Prayer

Share updated prayer requests. Ask one of the group members to close this session in prayer.

Session 12 Spiritual Warfare and the Eating Disordered

Introduction

Allow 10 Minutes

Opening Prayer

Thank God that in our struggle to live a new life which revolves around Jesus and His light, we are not left alone or defenseless. Even when Satan tries to destroy us, we have a defender who has already defeated the evil one.

Sharing Question

What have you learned about yourself this past week? How is your understanding of yourself growing as you participate in this group?

or

How is your relationship with food changing?

Personal response.

Self-Awareness

Allow 20 - 25 Minutes

During Session 2, we were reminded that "you will know the truth, and the truth will set you free" (John 8:32). **Truth** is both a process and a person, the person of Jesus Christ. John reminds us that "if the Son sets you free, you will be free indeed" (8:36). As believers, our position in Christ is secure; however, Satan constantly wars for our freedom. To attain victory over the darkness, we are instructed and encouraged to "put on the full armor of God so that you can take your stand against the devil's schemes" (Ephesians 6:11). Our "enemy the devil prowls around like a roaring lion looking for someone to devour" (1 Peter 5:8). For the eating-disordered individual, he "devours" through bondage to food and food-related issues.

In *Victory Over the Darkness*, Neil Anderson describes the two plans for *doing life*—Plan A (God's way) or Plan B (operating by our limited ability to reason).

> Plan B is based on our tendency to rationalize: *I don't see it God's way* or *I don't believe it.* Solomon urged us always to live God's way when he wrote: *Do not lean on your own understanding* (Plan B), but *in all your ways acknowledge Him* (Plan A) (Proverbs 3:5-6) (p. 158).

Anderson reminds us that "when you were born again, God gave you a new nature and you became a new person, but nobody pressed the *clear* button in your brain." He further clarifies that for the believer, spiritual warfare is a battle for the mind and "the essence of the battle for the mind is the conflict between Plan A, living God's way by faith, and Plan B, living man's way by following the impulses of the world, the flesh and the devil" (p. 159).

> You may feel like you are the helpless victim in this battle—but you are anything but helpless. In fact, YOU [capitalization added for emphasis] are the one who determines the winner in every skirmish between Plan A and Plan B (p. 160).

It is your choice how you fight. Your weapons must be divinely powerful (2 Corinthians 10:4) to win the battle to "demolish strongholds."

Stronghold: *A mentality impregnated with hopelessness that causes us to accept as unchangeable something that we know is contrary to the will of God.* —Rev. Ed Silvoso

How are strongholds developed? Negative thought patterns and beliefs are etched in our minds over time through either:

1. Repetition

   or

2. Onetime traumatic experiences

"An eating disorder is a spiritual stronghold." Do you agree or disagree? Explain your response.

Personal response.

Strongholds are developed as negative thought patterns which are etched into our minds. Review the negative thought patterns that *trigger* your eating disorder. Which of these negative thought patterns are the result of repetition or onetime traumatic experience?

Personal response.

If strongholds are *stored* in the mind, then the demolition of strongholds requires the "renewing of your mind" (Romans 12:2). (The Application section of this session will address and/or review strategies for the renewing of the mind.)

Spiritual Awareness Lead-In

The struggle for our lives is seen in John 10:10 through the words of Jesus. "The thief [Satan] comes only to steal and kill and destroy; I have come that they may have life, and have it to the full."

Spiritual-Awareness

Allow 20-25 Minutes

Satan's primary weapon is the **lie**. Your defense against him is **truth**. When you expose Satan's lie with God's truth, his power ceases.

Ephesians 6:10-18

How are we to access God's power to help us fight our spiritual war?

By putting "on the full armor of God."

What is the first piece of the full armor of God we are told to put on? Why do you think Paul chose to name it first?

The belt of TRUTH. Satan's primary weapon is the LIE. Our number one weapon against the lie is TRUTH. The belt of truth holds other pieces of armor in place.

List all of the pieces of armor. What does each represent?

Belt of Truth	God's truth defeats lies.
Breastplate of Righteousness	Satan often attacks our hearts, the seat of our emotions, self-worth, and trust. God's righteousness is the breastplate protecting and assuring our acceptance by God.
Footwear—The Gospel of Peace	The gospel's proclamation ensures true peace.
Shield of Faith	Faith protects us from Satan's flaming arrows.
Helmet of Salvation	The helmet protects us from doubting our salvation.
Sword of the Spirit, the Word of God	The is the only offensive weapon. The truth of the Word of God is our sure offense.

Which pieces of armor are you wearing? Which ones are missing?

Personal response.

Why is "full armor" necessary?

Unless we wear the FULL armor, Satan will sneak into our lives via an area of vulnerability.

Romans 12:2; Colossians 3:15-16; 1 Peter 1:13; 2 Corinthians 10:5; Philippians 4:6-7

According to these verses, what is your part in the battle for your mind?

1. Be transformed by renewing your mind.
2. To renew your mind, you must let the peace of Christ rule in your hearts and let the Word of Christ dwell richly in you.
3. Prepare your minds for action.

4. Take every thought captive for Christ.
5. Do not be anxious; present your requests to God and allow His peace to guard your heart and mind.

1 Corinthians 10:13; Galatians 5:1
What two "F's for the Fight" are identified in these verses?

God is **faithful**.
We are to stand **firm**.

Application

Allow 20 Minutes

Complete as many of the following as time permits:

1. Continue to apply the TRUTH system (from Session 2).

Ask a group member to volunteer an example of how they have used the TRUTH system this week **or** work through an example with the group.

2. 1 Corinthians 10:13 teaches us that God has provided a way of escape from every temptation. In *Victory Over the Darkness*, Neil Anderson uses a "Cathy" cartoon to illustrate (p 163):

Frame 1. I will take a drive but won't go near the grocery store.
Frame 2. I will drive by the grocery store but will not go in.
Frame 3. I will go in the grocery store but will not walk down the candy aisle.
Frame 4. I will walk down the candy aisle and look at the candy but not pick it up.
Frame 5. I will pick it up but not buy it.
Frame 6. I will buy it but not open it.
Frame 7. I will open it but not smell it.
Frame 8. I will smell it but not taste it.
Frame 9. I will taste it but not eat it.
Frame 10. I will eat, eat, eat, eat!!

When did Cathy lose the battle (i.e., what was her escape)?

Cathy lost the battle when she decided to take a drive. (The escape was in the first frame.) Rarely are we able to turn around after we have headed in the direction of Plan B thinking and behaving.

3. *Jehovah-Sabaoth*—The Lord of Hosts
If you have come to the end of your strength and need deliverance, turn to *Jehovah-Sabaoth,* the Lord of Hosts. This name of God meets failure and offers deliverance. In 1 Samuel 17:42-47, David called upon the Lord of Hosts and found deliverance: *You come against me with sword and spear and javelin, but I come against you in the name of the LORD Almighty* (v 45).

In 1 Samuel 1:1-3, 6-7, 10-11, Hannah called upon the Lord of Hosts and found deliverance.

Deliverance is available to you as well.
What do you need deliverance from? (Be specific.)

Personal response.

4. Warfare—or Discipline?
All too often Christians view anything negative that happens to them as "spiritual warfare." It is important to discern whether what we are experiencing is truly spiritual warfare or "disobedience." Galatians 6:7 reminds us that we will reap what we sow. A step in spiritual maturity is to recognize when God is disciplining us.

Carefully examine your life to determine if what you are experiencing is warfare or discipline.

5. Steps to Freedom in Christ

Are you ready to be free from the bondage of your eating disorder? (Remember John 5:6 when Jesus asked the invalid at the pool, "Do you want to get well?")

If so, inquire about "Freedom in Christ" ministries in your church or community or obtain a copy of *The Bondage Breaker* by Neil T. Anderson. Chapter 12 will guide you through the Seven Steps to Freedom in Christ.

Set a specific goal regarding putting on the full armor of Christ.

Update prayer requests.

Closing Prayer

Pray the following freedom prayer:

Lord, I renounce the lie that my value depends on my physical beauty, my weight, or my size. I renounce purging and/or restricting. I announce that only the blood of Christ cleanses me from sin and sets me free from bondage. I acknowledge that I am totally accepted by God in Christ, through my salvation, just as I am. In Jesus' name. Amen.

Session 13 Restoring the Temple: Tying the Recovery Process Together

Introduction

Allow 10 Minutes

Opening Prayer

Once again, invite the group to do the opening prayer. As you close out the prayer time, include a prayer that the Lord will use this last session to be a lasting and lifelong ministry and new life for all present.

Sharing Question

Which sessions of *Seeing Yourself in God's Image* have been most helpful to you? Explain. Which sections of the sessions have been most beneficial? Explain.

Personal responses.

What support/accountability do you need from the group to continue moving in a positive direction in your recovery from anorexia or bulimia?

Personal responses.

After completion of these 13 basic sessions of *Seeing Yourself in God's Image*, groups may choose to:

a. Recycle through the sessions.
b. Develop their own format for an ongoing group.
c. Disband but keep in contact with group members for support and accountability.

Self-Awareness

Allow 20 – 25 Minutes

For the last 12 sessions we have been examining anorexia and bulimia and the ten major emotional and perceptual characteristics that contribute to their development. Our last session is devoted to tying the recovery process together so that you have the tools necessary to make a commitment to "Restoring the Temple," your body, the temple of the Holy Spirit.

Note: You are the only one who can make that commitment. Remember the lame man at the pool in John 5. Before Jesus healed him, He asked, "Do you want to get well?"

Your life is the sum of the responses you have made to date. Through this study, God has made known to you what His desire is for your well-being—physically, emotionally, psychologically, and spiritually. The *choice* remains yours.

It is possible that you have become so accustomed to your bondage that you are resisting efforts to be free. The Israelites had been slaves in Egypt for four hundred years. They were not free. Moses had come to tell them how they could experience freedom, but they were more concerned with the "reactions of their taskmasters" than they were in obedience to God and the freedom obedience would bring. Freedom for them meant that Pharaoh would be angry and the Egyptians would attack them. Freedom did not seem to be worth the hardships they perceived they would have to endure.

When God frees us, there is often a price to pay. We can become so "comfortable" with the eating disorder and its bondage that we fear giving it up. As destructive as our eating behaviors may be, we prefer living with the familiar rather than being free to experience the unknown. Grieving the loss of the eating disorder, writing a "Dear John" letter to ED (i.e., saying good-bye to the eating disorder) is not easy. Have you been lulled into a comfortable relationship with your bondage to food and food-related issues? Do you fear change more than you rejoice in the freedom that only God can give? Are you willing to allow God to do what is necessary in order to free you? Are you ready to make a commitment?

Do I fully understand *commitment*? What is my definition of commitment?

Personal response

Review the drawbacks to the commitment of giving up anorexia or bulimia. (What would I lose by giving it up? Would I have to face anything or discover anything about myself?)

Review the good reasons for giving up the eating disorder.

Weigh the two lists. Are the good reasons worth the commitment? Do they outweigh the drawbacks that would have me continue to embrace my eating disorder?

What is "keeping me small" as a person rather than giving myself permission to mature in the Lord and "live out loud"?

It is time to redefine my commitment, making sure my head, heart, and soul all want to recover sufficiently to withstand the changes that might be forthcoming and uncomfortable.

I realize getting better often appears to be painful until I can see the light at the end of the tunnel (Jesus). If I choose to continue and pursue my commitment, it proves that I know I am worth the effort and I want to get well!

Encourage group members to make this commitment in writing for accountability with group members. (See also the "Saying Goodbye to ED and Hello to Jesus" activity in the Application section.)

Spiritual Awareness Lead-In

David said, "Commit your way to the LORD; trust in him and he will do this" (Psalm 37:5-6).

What will God do?

"He will make your righteousness shine like the dawn, the justice of your cause like the noonday sun"(Psalm 37:6).

Spiritual-Awareness

Allow 20-25 Minutes

Read the following verses as a prologue to the questions which follow:

Psalm 63:1-5
How does God honor thirst and longing for him?

This psalm reminds us that thirst is a longing for God and that our soul is satisfied with the richest of foods when it is satisfied by our relationship with God.

Knowing God and having Him reside within us is a "treasure of infinite value." Jesus likened this value to that of a pearl. The collector would readily sell everything he had in order to possess this one matchless pearl (Matthew 13:45-46). Your relationship with God places an immeasurable value on your life.

Colossians 2:2-3; Philippians 4:7; Ephesians 3:19-20
What do these verses tell us about our "infinite treasure"?

The treasures of God's wisdom and knowledge are available to us through Christ.

His incomprehensible peace surrounds our heart and mind.

When Jesus dwells in our life, everything available to Christ dwells within us.

Eugene Peterson in *Traveling Light* says:

> The world we live in is conspicuously and sadly lacking the *experience* of freedom. Since a free God is at the center of all existence and all creation and every creature issues from a free act, freedom and not necessity is always the deeper and more lasting reality. When I live in faith, I live freely. Like so many others who have chosen to live by faith, I find that it is a daily task to discriminate between the fantasies and the realities. I am convinced that people settle for far too little in matters of freedom (selected comments from pp. 9-15).

Reflecting on Paul's letter to the Galatians helps us ponder the free life. Below is a list of the chapters from *Traveling Light* and the *freedoms* the Apostle Paul discusses in his letter to the Galatians. Scriptural references to the Galatians passages are provided for each freedom.

Of which freedom(s) are you most in need? (Read the corresponding passages for Paul's encouragement.)

Select appropriate scriptures to read as a group or ask all group members to individually select and read the appropriate scriptures for their individual freedom needs.

1. Free for All
2. Free to Live (Galatians 1:1-5)
3. Free to Curse (Galatians 1:6-12)
4. Free to Change (Galatians 1:13-24)
5. Free to Resist (Galatians 2:1-10)
6. Free to Explore (Galatians 2:11-21)
7. Free to Think (Galatians 3:1-14)
8. Free to Fail (Galatians 3:15-27)
9. Free to Receive (Galatians 3:28-4:11)
10. Free to Trust (Galatians 4:12-31)
11. Free to Stand (Galatians 5:1-12)
12. Free to Love (Galatians 5:13-21)
13. Free to Create (Galatians 5:22-6:5)
14. Free to Give (Galatians 6:6-10)
15. Free to Die (Galatians 6:11-18)

Application

Allow 20 Minutes

Read Psalm 34:4-6.

How did the Psalmist David find freedom from his bondage?

He sought the Lord who delivered him from his fears and saved him from all of his troubles.

Memorize these scriptures for daily encouragement for ongoing recovery from anorexia or bulimia.

Affirmations

In preparation for ongoing affirmation of group members, as a group, develop a biblical affirmation alphabet. For each of the letters of the alphabet, identify an adjective descriptive of a woman who is "fearfully and wonderfully made" in God's image.

Personal response.

Examples:
A Alert to Satan's schemes
B Beautiful
C Complete in Christ

Use this alphabet to uphold one another on an ongoing basis.

A=
B=
C=
D=
E=
F=
G=
H=
I=
J=
K=
L=
M=
N=
O=
P=
Q=
R=
S=
T=
U=
V=
W=
X=
Y=
Z=

In addition to this group affirmation form, use the following forms (at the end of this session) in your ongoing recovery:

CHECKLIST

JOURNAL

MY REGULAR CHECKUP

Saying Good-bye to ED (Eating Disorder) and Hello to Jesus

As a closing activity for this support group, each participant is encouraged to write two brief letters—a good-bye letter to ED and a hello letter to Jesus—to indicate their commitment to being free from the bondage of anorexia or bulimia.

Time may only permit the beginnings of these letters. If so, group members are encouraged to complete these letters at home.

Update prayer requests.

Verify group members' names and telephone numbers (or e-mail addresses) who desire ongoing contact for support and accountability.

Closing Prayer

Open the prayer time for all beginning with a heartfelt prayer of thanksgiving to God for the people in the group, for their love for one another and for God, and for the deep love you have for them.

Checklist

If you will dedicate the time to do most of these activities daily, your chances for recovery will be stronger. As you accomplish each one, check it off on the daily worksheet. All in all, these should take a total of less than one hour per day. How much time did you usually dedicate to your preoccupation with food and weight in a day? Hang this chart where you will see it so it will remind you to work for yourself. Do not expect to do all the tasks every day or perfectly.

	SUN	MON	TUE	WED	THURS	FRI	SAT
Recite 10 things for which you are grateful.							
Read an uplifting or spiritually-based book.							
Ask the Lord to remove your urge to overeat/restrict. Ask to do the Lord's will instead.							
Call at least one supportive person.							
Pray.							
Write up tomorrow's eating plan.							
Follow and chart today's meal plan.							
Meditate for at least 10 minutes.							
Get your focus back on today only.							
Journal your feelings and thoughts.							
Sleep enough to be rested.							
Exercise 20-30 minutes, 5 days per week at least.							

Journal

It is important to keep a journal!

Even though it requires some effort, keeping a journal in chart form is one of the most important things we can do for ourselves. It helps us pinpoint the specific situations in which we want to work to behave more assertively. We suggest that you keep such a chart for at least a week so you can analyze your behavior patterns.

Situation and Thoughts	Physical Symptoms and Body Cues	How I Felt	My Behavior	What I Would Like to Have Done	Why I Did Not Do What I Wanted to Do

My Regular Checkup

- ✔ How do I feel today? (Pick at least three feelings from the feelings list on the next page or select other feelings of your own.)

- ✔ How am I *thinking* of myself today?

- ✔ What have I learned about myself this past week?

- ✔ The most challenging thing for me this week was __________.

- ✔ The major obstacle this week was ___________.

- ✔ What were your goals this week?

- ✔ On a scale of 1-10 (10 high), how was your ED recovery this week?

- ✔ Did you have any particular preoccupation with food this week that you would like to process with the group? If so, what?

Feelings

abandoned
accepted
adequate
adventurous
affected
afraid
alone
ambivalent
angry
animosity
anxious
apathetic
apprehensive
ashamed
awed
awkward
bewildered
bold
bored
brilliant
calm
captivated
caring
cautious
cheated
cheered
clownish
cold
comfortable
compelled
concerned
confident
congenial
constructive
contemptuous
content
cowardly
daring
dazed
defensive
defiant
depressed
desirous
despairing
despondent

disappointed
discontent
discouraged
distracted
disturbed
down
dull
eager
ecstatic
elated
embarrassed
empathic
empty
enchanted
encouraged
energized
envious
exasperated
excited
exhilarated
exploited
failure
fascinated
fearful
flighty
foolish
forlorn
free
frustrated
full
glad
goofy
graceful
graceless
grateful
great
guilty
gullible
gutsy
had
happy
hateful
helpless
hesitant
high

hopeful
hopeless
hostile
humble
hurt
impatient
important
indifferent
inferior
intolerant
irrational
irritated
jealous
joyful
jubilant
kind
knockdown
letdown
lonely
loved
lovely
miserable
natural
nervous
numb
obligated
overcome
overjoyed
overwhelmed
painful
peaceful
peppy
pious
pitiful
playful
pleased
poised
possessive
proud
provoked
pushed
put out
rational
refreshed
regretful

rejected
relieved
reluctant
remorseful
resented
resigned
respectable
revengeful
robbed
satisfied
secure
selfish
self-pitying
shy
sick
snappy
stubborn
stunned
stupid
successful
sucked in
suffering
superior
surprised
surrender
suspicious
sympathetic
tired
tranquil
trapped
uncomfortable
understood
uneasy
unhappy
unloved
unmasked
unsure
unworthy
used
warm
weary
witty
wonderful
worthy

References

American Psychiatric Association, *Diagnostic and Statistical Manual of Mental Disorders, Fourth Edition,* Washington, DC, American Psychiatric Association, 1994.

Anderson, Neil T., *The Bondage Breaker,* Harvest House Publishers, Eugene, OR, 1990.

______, *Victory Over the Darkness,* Regal Books, Ventura, CA, 1990.

Bray-Garretson, Helen, and Kaye V. Cook, *Chaotic Eating: A Guide to Recovery,* Zondervan, Grand Rapids, MI, 1992.

Burns, David D., M.D., *Feeling Good: The New Mood Therapy,* Avon, New York, 1992.

Carter, Les, and Frank Minirth, *The Freedom From Depression Workbook,* Thomas Nelson Publishers, Nashville, TN, 1995.

Garner, David M., and Paul E. Garfinkel, *Handbook of Treatment for Eating Disorders 2nd Ed,* The Guilford Press, New York, NY, 1997.

McCormick, Denise, Terry Kottman, and Jeff Ashby, "Conceptualization and Treatment of the Bulimic Client from an Adlerian Perspective," *Individual Psychology,* 52, 406-410.

Matzat, Don, *Christ Esteem,* Harvest House, Eugene, OR, 1990.

Miles, Donald, *Understanding Depression: Overcoming Despair Through Christ, Facilitator's Guide,* Turning Point Ministries, Inc., Chattanooga, TN, 1998.

Moorehead, Bob, *Counsel Yourself and Others From the Bible,* Multnomah Books, Sisters, OR, 1994.

O'Neill, Cherry Boone, and Dan O'Neill, *Living on the Border of Disorder,* Bethany House, Minneapolis, MN, 1992.

Peterson, Eugene, *Traveling Light,* InterVarsity Press, Downers Grove, IL, 1982.

Pipher, Mary, *Hunger Pains: The Modern Woman's Tragic Quest for Thinness,* Ballantine Books, New York, NY, 1995.

Poinsett, Brenda, *Why Do I Feel This Way?,* Navpress, Colorado Springs, CO, 1996.

Siegel, Michele, Judith Brisman, and Margot Weinshel, *Surviving An Eating Disorder: Strategies for Family and Friends,* Harper Perennial, New York, NY, 1997.

Thompson, Marcia, and Sue Michel Janssen, *Circles of Love: A Map to Wellness,* Christian Counseling Ministries, Inc., Green Bay, WI, 1996.

Chris Thurman, *The Lies We Believe,* Thomas Nelson, Nashville, TN, 1989.

______, *The Lies We Believe Workbook,* Thomas Nelson, Nashville, TN, 1995.

______, *The Truths We Must Believe,* Thomas Nelson, Nashville, TN, 1991.

Vath, Raymond E., *Counseling Those With Eating Disorders,* Word Books, Waco, TX, 1986.

Vredevelt, Pam, et. al., *The Thin Disguise,* Thomas Nelson, Nashville, TN, 1992.